The Americas

A Captivating Guide to the History of the Continents of North and South America, Starting from the Olmecs through the Maya and Aztecs to European Colonization and Independence Movements

Free Bonus from Captivating History
(Available for a Limited time)

Hi History Lovers!

Now you have a chance to join our exclusive history list so you can get your first history ebook for free as well as discounts and a potential to get more history books for free! Simply visit the link below to join.

Captivatinghistory.com/ebook

Also, make sure to follow us on Facebook, Twitter and Youtube by searching for Captivating History.

Contents

Introduction

The one-character trait that sometimes surpasses the human instinct for survival is curiosity. When humans discovered an entire hemisphere that lay beyond their own Eastern Hemisphere, the race was on.

What opportunities would these new lands hold? Surely, a small country in Europe could wield the power of an empire if it could claim these new lands in the Americas. After all, there was new fertile land in these Americas, the lure of wealth, the entertainment of exciting wildlife, productive vegetation, and the marvelous treasures that shone and glittered. "So daily do I send these praises coming forth in the garb of our ancestors: I shine; I glitter," prayed the ancients. The cry for gold overcame all the people's mortal fears. It echoed in 1528 in the search for the ethereal El Dorado, in 1632 in Venezuela, and in the frigid Yukon in 1896.

The countries came and claimed and clashed as they tried to mix and meld. Instead, they found themselves caught in the dialectic of opposing sides, caught in a game of tug-of-war over acres of plains and pampas, sand and stones, mountains and mesas.

It was the rush of civilizations. In 1494, two headstrong countries—Portugal and Spain—"divided" up this grand New World between them with a ludicrous agreement called the Treaty of Tordesillas. It was ignored by the French, the Dutch, and the English. The indigenous tribes, who had controlled the lands before the Europeans descended upon them, looked upon the intruders first as visitors, then disease carriers, and then enemies of the lands that they insisted were their right to own. Settlements and civilizations rose and fell, like the Maya of the Yucatan Peninsula, the Aztecs of Mexico, the conquistadors of old, and the masked warriors who made greed their motive.

The Americas is a collage of differences and similarities. Civilizations, like the waves at the shore, will ebb and flow throughout history. They might rise and fall, but more often than not, they will not fall without leaving behind their legacies, upon which life is built.

You will see in these pages that history may repeat itself, but there is always progress and change. Like the sun that always rises, there will always be new days where the indomitable spirit of humankind surpasses its own dreams. This is shown in the story of the people who lived and ventured to the Americas.

This story is massive, and for that reason, it is important to note that not everything can be covered. Many events that deserve an entire book on their own will be given a brief summary. However, this book is a great way to whet your appetite for more information, and hopefully, you will be able to do further research on the topics that pique your interest. The book first touches upon the major ancient civilizations of Mexico and South America before being divided into sections on South and North America. The information, for the most part, is told chronologically in their respective sections for easier readability.

Chapter 1 – The Olmecs: The Rubber People (1500–400 BCE)

Patiently, the ancient artisan bent below a tubule he had shoved into the trunk of a rubber tree (CASTILLA ELASTICA) to collect the milky fluid (latex) as it oozed from the fifty-foot tree looming above the forest canopy. After taking his pail to the campsite, the man carried it gingerly to his work area. Then he took some of the latex, molded it into a ball-shape, and let it harden on a rock. He then stirred up the rest of the latex with the squeezed juices of ground-up vines that are related to the Morning Glory plants of today. Next, he flattened the mixture with a stone rolling-pin device and cut the irregular piece into strips. Each strip was progressively wrapped around the rubber ball core. These balls were of various sizes, from that of a volleyball to slightly larger than a tennis ball. Since they were made of solid rubber, they were all relatively heavy. The hard-working man brought his handiwork to the ball games and tribal celebrations in the towns carved out of the dense jungles of Mesoamerica.

Mesoamerica is Central America, that strip of land connecting the continents of North America and South America. The Sierra Madre Mountains in the north and south created highland areas that were relatively arid. The lowlands were a very green area, heavily canopied with very tall trees. The moist black soil was fertile and wet. A constant "hiss" emanated from the ground, produced by locusts and oversized insects that were rapidly snapped up by the wild mice and rats. Giant vines hung from the trees, as well as snakes, so the cautious hunter kept a skin-like "scarf" on his head.

As the hunters stealthily tiptoed through the jungles, the heavy footfall of the jaguar wove in between the tree-trunks, in search of prey once night had fallen. The jaguar was a magnificent spotted mammal that hunted crocodiles, turtles, snakes, monkeys, tapirs, and peccaries. Tapirs and peccaries, which are very common in the rainforest, are pig-like animals that congregate near waterholes. The hunters of Mesoamerica tracked the paths of jaguars because they consumed the same prey.

The Olmec people occupied the center of Mesoamerica. Their culture is called a "mother culture," meaning that other civilizations in the area spawned from that one. For example, there were nearly identical practices within the Maya civilization that paralleled that of the Olmecs. Their northern shore was along the Gulf of Mexico in the portion known as Veracruz; one of the most important cities of the Olmecs was what is now the modern-day city of San Lorenzo, which was located about midway across the isthmus. A segment of the southern area of the Olmecs was comfortably inland in a territory free of flooding. The eastern portion of the Olmec state was located in current-day Tabasco.

Most ethologists now believe that the earliest inhabitants of this fiercely challenging land were Africans. Theoretically, the first humans to reach the American continent came perhaps 20,000 years ago, and it has been suggested that they either came from Africa or the Far East and migrated across a "land-bridge" made of ice connecting northeastern Asia (Russia) and western Alaska known as Beringia. Due to intermarriage over the centuries, some of these early inhabitants may have descended from peoples in Siberia.

The phenomenon of the land bridge occurred because the ice sheets over the northern part of the globe sucked up much of the earth's water, lowering the sea level by 300 feet. Within less than 1,000 years, the earliest human ancestors arrived in Mesoamerica.

Considering the geography of the Pacific region, it is only remotely possible that these peoples arrived by sea, but, if they did, they would have been of Polynesian ancestry and had high cheekbones. Geologists have speculated that there was a climactic change severe enough in Africa and China to trigger this exodus. For many miles, these ancient peoples trekked northeast through Asia and crossed the land bridge. It's logical to assume they settled in Mesoamerica, as it had the tropical and subtropical climate they were accustomed to.

Trade

Trade flourished along the waterways of the Olmec territory. Most of the items used were jade jewelry, pottery, and ornate earrings. "Olmec blue" was a bluish-tinted jade that was unique to this area. Semi-precious stones like jade and turquoise were also traded and used for medicinal purposes. Treatments for the eye included poultices made from turquoise or jade, and healing stones were utilized for headaches and backaches. These stones were also used for ornamentation, and the wealthier wore beautiful necklaces. Although it was less prevalent, gold and silver artifacts were also found. Many jeweled pieces were considered talismans to protect their wearers from evil spirits. Obsidian was used not only for mirrors but was also used to create arrowheads for the spears used in hunting.

The Olmec Gods

Religion solidifies a society, and the Olmec created their religion around their respect for the jaguar. Because he was a creature of the night, the jaguar god, called the "Were-jaguar," was the god of the underworld. When anthropomorphized, the jaguar god is portrayed as having a downturned mouth and a fierce expression. Sometimes, the figures of the jaguar were carved out of stone and were heavily-toothed, demonstrating ferocity. Some archeologists indicate that their main god was the Were-jaguar or the rain spirit. Because water was so vital for the life of these hardy peoples, the rain spirit was a central figure.

Art analysts have examined the Olmec figures found in Rio Chiquito, Fuente, and Potrero Nuevo and have theorized that they might denote copulation between humans and the were-jaguar. This act also gave rise to the "were-babies" sometimes seen in their art. Olmecs may have believed that their gods and rulers were the descendants of the sacred jaguar.

A beautiful statue dated around 1000 BCE carved out of greenstone was found in Veracruz, Mexico. It is a tender portrayal of a youth or a young woman holding a were-jaguar baby in their arms. The sad and pleading expression is still pronounced even after all these years. The jaguar is limp, perhaps as a symbol of the afterlife.

The Olmecs had a cluster of gods. The Olmec Dragon was a crocodile god, which represented the earth plane. It represented agriculture and fertility, as the Olmecs were not only hunters but also farmers, who created clearings in their vast forests and raised maize and beans.

The Bird Monster of the ancient Olmecs represented the skies and was often used as a symbol to demonstrate power and prominence. The Olmecs felt it represented their revered rulers, as it was often found embroidered on their garments. The quetzal is an iridescent blue bird with a red belly and a very long blue tail, which is still common to the region, and it was most likely used as a model for this god.

The Fish Monster, or "Shark Monster," represented the underworld. In the town of San Lorenzo, there is a giant representation of the Fish Monster—a god with many sharp teeth. Archeologists have theorized that it is associated with one of the creation myths, which depicts a man who lost a limb to this enormous creature, with the missing limb leading to the formation of landmasses on the water.

The Maize God symbolized the primary staple crop of the Olmecs. Historians have indicated that their rulers were responsible for maintaining the steady production of the crop, and the Maize

God was their aide in doing so. If a seasonal crop failed, the leader was held responsible and was often exiled for that failure, as it meant he wasn't making the proper offerings to the Maize God, who responded with displeasure by punishing the people.

Corn, a community crop, could be grown in cleared patches throughout the jungle. A solitary plant would not grow alone, and the cornfield had to be carefully tended. The corn silk was used for baskets, hats, and clothing. The children were often told mythical stories, similar to parables, to reinforce good work habits. A favorite tale was that of the grandmother and the twins who were given the responsibility of taking care of the cornfield. They were told that if they neglected their task, the evil spirits would come, and they would be required to go through an ordeal to make matters right again.

The Water God was often shown in Olmec art as well. The god was depicted as a chubby infant, reminiscent of a child who was satiated by its mother's milk. Water was essential to life, and the rainforests were real natural manifestations of its force. Olmecs consumed shrimp, conch, squid, and clams. Some were caught along the sunny blue shores of the Gulf of Mexico, and others were freshwater clams found in the inland lakes and waterways. The Olmecs would wander near these inland rivers and bodies of water, and once they spotted a small pile of broken clam shells, it was relatively easy to follow the narrow animal trails and locate wildlife that could be trapped and eaten.

The Feathered Serpent represented the dual nature of the deities and was one of their most important gods. It can be found on an elaborately designed stone stele, showing the crested head of a serpent coiled artistically around a godly figure with embellishments in relief. The Feathered Serpent is also depicted in Monument 19, found in Villahermosa, Mexico. The site, La Venta, is in Tabasco, where there are many monumental buildings, including a pyramid, plazas, and platforms. The site contains countless numbers of "offerings" to the gods, such as jade artifacts, polished mirrors made of obsidian and iron ore, and serpentine blocks. Serpentinite is a dark green gemstone. The color green was associated with snakes since so many of the water snakes in Mesoamerica were (and still are) green.

The Mesoamerican Ball Game

The Olmecs were said to have first invented the ritual game that used a rubber ball, a game that was mostly played by the nobles and elites. The practice spread to other Mesoamerican cultures, like the Maya and the Aztecs, who refined the rules. Two teams competed, and it was believed that the sport represented the struggle between good and evil. Olmec courts were rather primitive and varied from an "I" shape to a "T" shape. The objective was to get the ball to the opposite end of the court through a stone hoop. Methods of scoring differed from one time period to the next. It was similar to volleyball, with the exception that hands could not be used. Only hips, legs, and elbows were engaged to keep the ball in motion. In some cases, the losing team was sacrificed to the gods, and its players used bloodletting rituals, like the piercing of tongues or testicles.

Diet

Besides the nutrition obtained from the consumption of meat from pork and rodent-related animals, as well as fish and shellfish, the people supplemented their food with bean vegetables, bread, and sweets.

Cornmeal, which was made from maize, brought about the use of dough. Consequently, flatbreads like tortillas were invented, and hot peppers were used to create a spread. Crops of hybrid white corn gave rise to the discovery of popcorn.

Cacao trees grew wild in Mesoamerica, and chocolates were made from the seeds. This chocolate was more bittersweet than sweet, and the chocolate was more like dark chocolate. They also made beverages from it, so these ancient folks enjoyed hot cocoa! Mesoamerica was ideal for the growth of stevia, a small shrub with sweet leaves. It grew wild in the less humid soils there, and the people made sweeteners from it. Agave plants also grew wild in these lowland regions, and sweeteners could be made from them as well.

The Colossal Heads

Scattered through the dense forests of the Olmecs are seventeen giant heads carved in relief. They are all about nine feet tall, and the weights range from six to forty tons. Each one is made of basalt, an igneous rock, which had been transported with great effort from the Sierra de la Tuxtlas Mountains along the coast of the Gulf in Veracruz. It is more than likely that the El Vigia volcano in that mountain range produced the basalt. The faces have African features, providing further evidence that Africa may have well been the origin of these people. Most of the statues have some kind of domed headpiece with a decorated band across the forehead, and it's been suggested that they were wearing the headbands of team players in their ball games. Some of the ancient historians indicate that these were the faces of the various rulers of the Olmec people. Their expressions are mostly placid, but there are a few that are smiling. However, it's worthy of note that each face is distinctly different. Researchers have discovered that they were, at one time, brightly painted.

The Olmecs were very talented sculptors, and they left many artifacts behind that reveal a softness and fluidity of form. The fetal form was also displayed in some of the figures. Some researchers refer to them as "dwarfs," and since dwarfs played an important role in Olmec mythology, some believe that there might have been a race of dwarfs present in Olmec society.

Water Drainage

Water was the most prized commodity in the highland areas of the Olmecs. The lowland areas were vulnerable to flooding, so the Olmecs developed aqueducts to direct the rainwater around their essential buildings, especially their temples. The drainage system consisted of many conduits, and there was evidence that they enjoyed public baths.

Measurement

Hematite is an iron-based ore that has magnetic properties, and it was used to create primitive compasses to determine one's location and for the building and placement of farm fields. Artifacts of polished hematite were found in Mesoamerica, and excavations of public sites such as arenas show geometric exactness. This directional component permitted ancient planners to take advantage of sunlight and shade to build the stone bleachers in such a way as to allow for the best visibility and avoid the glaring sun in spectators' eyes. Some theorists also indicate that hematite was used for geomancy, that is, for divination. The Olmec discovery of hematite used as a lodestone predates the Chinese, who were once thought of as the first group to discover it.

Historians have speculated that the Olmec civilization was the first to develop the calendar. They have also been credited with the invention of the number "zero," which definitively marked a milestone in early mathematics.

Writing

The Olmecs had a writing system composed of 62 glyphs. The written word ran horizontally, which is unusual, as most of the earliest known writing is vertical. The first known artifact displaying a writing system in the Americas was the Cascajal Block. It was found in San Lorenzo, Veracruz, and is evidence of the fact that the Olmecs invented the first written language in the Western Hemisphere.

Pyramids

In Mesoamerica, the pyramid wasn't used as a burial site for its venerated rulers; instead, it was used as a monument to a deity or a ruler. It was initially built like a step pyramid. Due to erosion, the 112-foot high Great Pyramid in San Lorenzo is now mound-shaped.

The top of the Great Pyramid may have been flat at one time. Although much is based on conjecture, archeologists believe that fabulous altars were constructed on the top. Crowds of anticipatory people would gather at the pyramid and watch as their shamans burned incense and prayed to the gods for good harvests. Some have proposed the theory that the Olmecs may have been involved in the sacrifice of infants to the gods, but there is no substantiating evidence of that. It is true, though, that other Mesoamerican cultures engaged in human sacrifice. In fact, the losing teams would sometimes be sacrificed. On occasion, the Olmec team forced their prisoners to play the ball game to the death.

The Decline of the Olmecs

Without a written record, it is difficult to establish what led to the disappearance of the Olmec civilization. A large amount of volcanic rock in the area of their towns could be evidence that a volcanic eruption from a chain of volcanoes could have wiped out the human habitation in the region. Severe climatic change was often responsible for the disappearance of certain geographically distinct territories as well. That may have led to widespread crop failures, leading to starvation. Because the latest identified artifacts were dated to around 400 BCE, this is the approximate year cited as the end of the Olmec period.

Chapter 2 – The Maya: The K'iche' People (3000 BCE–1511 CE)

The Maya were people who originated in Asia. Like the Olmecs, they traversed across Beringia, the land bridge between the Eastern and Western Hemispheres. They then settled in today's Yucatan Peninsula of Mexico, Guatemala, Belize, and portions of Honduras and El Salvador. It was a wondrous land, heavily forested, and boasted extremely fertile areas suitable for farming. The regions in Yucatan were low-lying, and the extreme southern areas were mountainous, as they are a part of the Sierra Madre mountain chain. The people who settled there were called the K'iche' people. The term "K'iche'" means "many trees." The earliest known archeological artifacts of these people date back to 2600 BCE.

The earliest known text of the history of the K'iche' was the *Popol Vuh*, meaning "Book of the K'iche' People." It was initially passed along through oral tradition and later recorded by several historians, including Father Ximénez in the early 18th century. There were other ancient sources as well, which account for variations in the names of their gods and the myths surrounding the creation of the world and the history of the Maya civilization as a whole.

The Maya people believed that there was one great tree, the World Tree, growing in the heart of their land. It was represented by the giant ceiba tree, a straight-trunked tree that towered over all the others in the forest canopy of the Maya lands. According to their creation myths, that tree connected the sky to the earth. The earth was rooted through the trunk of the World Tree in the underworld, which was called Xibalba. Hunab Ku was the god of heaven, which was called Tamoanchan, while Ah Puch, referred to as Itzamna in ancient texts, was the god of Xibalba.

The Maya had a pantheon of gods, and as many as 165 of them were in control of different aspects of the known world. Hunab Ku was the high god and the father of the twins Hunahpu and Xbalanque. The twins represent the duality seen in nature and cosmogony—day and night, sky and earth, life and death. Many mythological tales spun from stories about the trials of the twins, incorporating those which explained the birth of a new age and the creation of the sun and the moon, given to Kinich Ahau and Ixchel to rule, respectively. Ixchel was also the goddess of love, childbirth, and the arts.

Two of the primary myths explained what the Maya found when they settled in Mesoamerica. One accounted for the climate and the other for the creation of humankind.

Climate/Geography

Huracan, a powerful creator god of the Maya, was the primordial breath, the god of the winds and the storms. Hurricanes were common in Mesoamerica and tended to be frequent in the lowland areas, which much of the Maya territory was. The northeastern areas had heavy rainfall, while the northwest was dry. This tremendous difference in the climate created a karst environment, or an area typified by bedrock that has been worn away underneath by water. That created cenotes, or massive sinkholes. The underground waters also produced caves and springs, which the Maya territory was punctuated with. The Maya believed that the cenotes led to the underworld, and indeed, they seem to give that appearance. Representations of Al Puch, the god of the underworld, feature a non-descript face with a wide-open mouth, sometimes portrayed with teeth, which symbolized a cenote. He was there to swallow up evildoers and accept the offerings of the people. Some of the cenotes were relatively shallow and could be used to irrigate the fields, but there were also extremely deep and dangerous cenotes. Some of those served religious purposes, such as being the repository for offerings to the deities. The Maya did practice human sacrifice, and human bones have been found at the bottom of some of these wells and pits.

The Maya territory, as mentioned above, also included mountains, which can be found in current-day central Mexico. This territory, even today, is semi-arid and constitutes part of the Sierra Madre mountain chain. There are four active volcanoes located in the highlands. The ancient text Chilam Balam, dating back to 2600 BCE, refers to a tremendous volcanic eruption, in which "a fiery rain fell, and ashes fell, and their great serpent god, Kukulkan, was ravished from the heavens."

This area was plagued by earthquakes and mudslides due to the extreme variation in the water table. The twins Hunahpu and Xbalanque had the task of protecting the Maya from earthquakes. Also, eruptions, tropical storms, and natural disasters occurred in this weather-beaten area and were causes for the people to make offerings to their deities. One of the creator deities, Huracan, gave rise to light (Cakulha-Hurakan) and, in conjunction with Chaac, the god of rain, he brought storms and lightning (Chipi-Cakulha). There were many arid areas that needed rain, and the people relied upon the intervention of the rainmaker gods to bring about a balance of these natural forces.

The Creation of Man and Maize

The creator deities wanted a helpmate with a spiritual soul, so they created humankind. It was a challenging task, and they had to try three times to get it right. On the first attempt, they created a human of mud. The mud wasn't satisfactory and washed away. Then they created men of wood, like wooden manikins. However, they failed to infuse those with souls. Having no spirit life within, they were goalless and turned into "howlers," or monkeys. Then the gods took an ear of maize. With some effort, they made a dough from it and fashioned that dough into human beings. The people made of maize were successful and were pleasing to the gods because they grew and reproduced, covering the land. Some of the mythological accounts attribute the name Hun Hunahpu to the maize god, while other versions use both a male and female version of the maize god, calling the male Yum Kaax and the female Hun-Nal-Ye. Some stories indicate that Yum Kaax was not only the god of maize but also the god of plants and animals.

Around 2600 BCE, the first maize plants grown in Mesoamerica were raised in an area called Cuell, located in modern-day Belize. This area shows evidence of continual farming and settlements, dating to around 1800 BCE. In the land of the Maya, maize would grow in both the lowlands and the highlands. Usually, it was grown in patches and would be interspersed with beans, chili peppers, and squash. The silk and leaves from the plants were used for baskets and hats, as people needed to keep their heads shaded to prevent excessive perspiration and subsequent dehydration in the subtropical climate. Pottery fragments also date back to that period, and the people used earthen kilns to fashion figures as well as pottery.

Some of the Maya territories were in areas where there was flooding. To grow crops in Yucatan, it was necessary to build aqueducts and create an irrigation system. The lowlands of the central area likewise needed to be terraced to prevent excessive flooding, and the mountainous areas were also challenging, as it was necessary to prevent erosion from the water runoff. So, to grow maize and other crops, the Maya built terraces. Their step pyramids are a good reflection of their agricultural techniques.

The Maya were also some of the earliest people to develop elevated roadways. Some roads were built within the forested areas, thus allowing passage through the jungles. In the thick forests, these roads rose as high as eight feet above the ground. Others were built to be above the flooded lowlands so people and their carts could traverse safely. Because the roads were constructed primarily of limestone, weeds and wild grasses were kept to a minimum.

Maya Society and Structure

Between the years 1500 BCE and 400 CE, the population was split into groups, those who settled in Yucatan and its environs and those who settled in the southern areas of current-day Guatemala, which was closer to the Pacific Ocean.

The prehistorical ruins of cities have been discovered, which seem to indicate that the Maya were segmented into a group of city-states. In the years spanning 1500 BCE to 1511 CE, each city-state had its own king and queen.

The gods of the *Popol Vuh* predicted that the day was coming when the people would be less dependent upon the gods, meaning they could not automatically call upon the deities to resolve their difficulties through magic and myth. The *Popol Vuh* said, "The gods are alarmed that beings who were merely manufactured by them should have divine powers, so they decided, after their usual dialogue, to put a fog on human eyes. Next, they make four wives for the four men, and from these couples come the leading lineages." They were, therefore, considered the parents of the civilization, and the rulers of the Maya were descended from them. They were "god-like," as opposed to being considered gods. The rulers weren't always men; some were women, but most of the time, the women were in charge when the head king wasn't of age or when he was away on a trade mission or at war.

This was the Classic Period of the Maya, whose civilization can be divided into three periods:

Pre-classic - 2000 BCE to 250 CE

Classic - 250 CE to 900 CE

Postclassic - 900 CE to 1500 CE

In an area excavated near Guatemala City, archeologists discovered stone platforms, presumably used for an acropolis of sorts with markets. Inside some of the mounds, two very ornate tombs were found, replete with stone replications of prior rulers of the polity. Stelae with insignias marking the graves of the elites were also found throughout the area, but few survive today.

Very early glyphs were carved into several mounds at what appears to be a monument in the Maya city of Kaminaljuyu. They highlighted either a religious belief or were a representation of the economic activity of the various social classes. The classes consisted of the royal lineage and elites, the priests, the middle class, who produced the main products of the Maya, and the lower classes. Their homes were made of wattle and daub, a combination of sticks adhered together with a wet mixture of clay, animal dung, and straw. The elites and the middle classes worked together to produce goods and horticultural items for the people and trade. The elites and the middle class lived near each other, but the lower classes were relegated to living on the city's outskirts.

Deadly Games

The Maya had highly decorated step pyramids that were used as temples and for festive celebrations. In this central area, fifteen ball courts were unearthed, and it was believed that these ball games served two purposes: a reenactment of a myth or a challenge between the Maya and their enemies.

The ball games could be ceremonial or bloody. They were based on the Maya myth of the hero twins of Hunab Ku, Hunahpu and Xbalanque. As the mythical tale tells, the two boys disturbed the lords of Xibalba, the underworld. As a result, the twins had to play many deadly games with the young lords of Xibalba. The twins overcame the many ruses set up by the lords, and they deliberately lost some of the games to make their opponents overly confident. Then, toward the end of the tournament, they overcame the challenges of the Jaguar House by avoiding slaughter and the Fire House by coming out unharmed. In the challenge of the Bat House, Hunahpu was decapitated by the bat god, Camazotz. However, the supernatural powers of the hero twins surpassed that of the evil lords of Xibalba, so the head was temporarily replaced with that of a gourd and then exchanged for Hunahpu's original head.

After the game, the chief lords of Xibalba wanted the miracle to be performed on them, but Hunahpu and Xbalanque didn't resurrect them again. They indicated that Xibalba was no longer a realm to be respected, and they left. After that, Hunahpu and Xbalanque rose to the higher heavens and became the sun and the moon.

The Game Itself: Ulama

There were two teams who played against each other with a rubber ball. The ball itself could weigh as much as ten pounds. The players had to keep the ball in play by hitting it with their hips, thighs, or upper arms, never with their hands or feet. A point system established the winners and losers. It was sometimes even fought as a proxy for war. At times, it was fought between the Maya and their enemies, in which case the losers were sacrificed. On the other hand, some of the religious ritual games resulted in the decapitation of the winning captain, who went straight into the heaven world as a reward.

The game wasn't always played as a blood sport. Smaller rubber balls were found as well as smaller courts, which were perhaps meant for children.

Classic Period: Palenque

Early signs of trade among the early Maya showed up in the southern Pacific region, where obsidian mirrors and jade jewelry were found. There was also an Olmec artifact located in Maya territory, which indicates that some trade was conducted between the two civilizations. Trade was conducted between the great city-states, such as Palenque, who traded prolifically with the smaller city-states of Tikal, Pomona, and Tortuguero. Palenque was in the central northern area of the Yucatan Peninsula, now known as the state of Chiapas, Mexico.

The most noted ruler during the Classic Period was K'inich Janaab Pakal I, also known as Pacal. His mother, Sak K'uk, ruled for three years, from 612 to 615 CE, until her son could assume control. It was the first task of any new ruler to prove his lineage and partial divinity, as the rulers were understood to be those who worked in conjunction with the gods to bring prosperity to the region through the balance of nature and man. To make his reign legitimate and sanctioned by the gods, Pacal built the Temple of Inscriptions in 675. It was designed as a step pyramid with an altar on top. Archeologists discovered that there was a lower structure within the central portion that descended into the tomb of Pacal, which was located within a subterranean grotto carved out of rock and ice. When the excavations were completed, it revealed that the lower floors opened into a fairytale-like world of stalactites and stalagmites. On the walls, there were carvings decorated with jade stones, depicting scenes of Pacal emerging out of Xibalba, the underworld. He was adorned as the maize god and was shown ascending into the heaven world. Displayed on the outside of the sarcophagus is the World Tree puncturing through to the heaven world with a bird god to accompany him.

From archeological evidence, it seems that the rival city-state of Toniná, located near Palenque, may have attacked Palenque around 711 CE. Pacal was captured by Toniná, and so, historians debate as to whether or not the human remains found in the tomb are his.

Toniná

Although the two city-states of Palenque and Toniná were ongoing rivals, the first monument at Toniná appears to have been erected around 633 CE during the Classic Period. It had seven tiers, upon which the altar was located. One side of it was called the Palace of the Frets (or Palacio de las Grecas). The inscriptions around the walls are mostly serpentine in nature to honor the snake god Kukulkan. Kukulkan was depicted as a feathered serpent, so avian features were also present.

To the front of the Toniná monument was the Temple of the Earth Monsters, which had an altar on top showing the head of the Earth Monster. Below the head was a gaping hole to represent his wide-opened mouth. This form was inspired by the topology of the karst countryside, which created the great sinkholes, or cenotes, that were believed to be entrances to the underworld. It was taught that the divine rulers could enter and leave the underworld at will. Their last trip after death was believed to be a journey into the underworld, and from there, they went to the heights of heaven. The stone walls had images of the water gods to symbolize the fact that many of the underground cenotes contained water.

In the fifth terrace of the Toniná monument is the giant Frieze of the Bird Dancers. They symbolized not only the celebrations but also the ball games. After all, the ball games did not hold the connotation that today's games have—they were serious affairs. Friezes of the mythological ball game fought between the lords of the heaven and the lords of the underworld are depicted on the friezes and show a segment of the conflict between one of the sons of the great god Hunab Ku and the lords of the underworld of Xibalba.

The people of Toniná, along with their ally, the city-state of Calakmul, were at war in the 680s. In 688, the Toniná ruler (name unknown) captured the king of Palenque, K'inich Kan Bahlam II. The following ruler of Toniná, K'inch B'aaknal Chaak, forced the Palenque prisoners to participate in their bloody life and death games.

By the year 909, there were no more leaders listed in Toniná on the steles or in the carvings. Toniná was in an isolated area, and the city-state went into a severe decline after that, both economically and socially. It was supplanted by other civilizations in the future, but the reasons for its final decline are unknown.

Postclassic Period: Chichen Itza

The term "Chichen Itza" means "mouth of the well." It is an ancient city located in the Yucatan Peninsula and was built alongside a giant natural sinkhole. These sinkholes, or cenotes, were caused by the weakening and subsequent collapse of bedrock when underground waters increased in volume. There is disagreement as to the date for the actual founding of Chichen Itza, but it is generally agreed that it was built between 550 to 800 CE and thrived until 900 CE. Because it was built, rebuilt, and added to throughout the centuries, different styles are displayed. The term "Toltec" has been used by researchers to refer to artisans and/or mystics who lived after 900 CE in the towns of Tula, Hidalgo, and Chichen Itza. Some say the Toltecs were a military tribe, while others say the Toltecs were members of a splinter group of believers who followed the mythological figure Quetzalcoatl. Their carvings differ somewhat from that of the earlier Maya, but they appear to have blended the previous style with their own quite well.

Along with its shrines and altars, Chichen Itza was a complex of many structures that served various purposes. It had temples, ball courts, administrative buildings, and platforms for markets. The cenotes provided a ready water supply year-round.

On the north side, there is a giant sinkhole called Cenote Sagrado (Sacred Cenote), which, when dredged by archeologists, showed collections of jade, silver, gold, and human bones. The markings on the human bones show that the people who were sacrificed were slaughtered first before being thrown into the pit, the entrance to the "underworld." Some of the bones are those of children. It was said that some of the people offered their children up in sacrifice on the eve of battle in order to assure victory.

There are four significant clusters of buildings in Chichen Itza: the Great North Platform, the Central Group, the Osario group, and the Old Chichen (the latter isn't open to visitors).

On the Great North Platform stands the Kukulkan Pyramid (El Castillo), which was dedicated to the serpent god. During the autumnal and vernal equinoxes, the sun creates a shadow on the steps of the pyramid that looks like a snake. This platform also has a shrine to the planet Venus, which was the stellar patron of Kukulkan. Maya astronomers and astrologers plotted the path of Venus through the year with amazing accuracy. Both Kukulkan and Venus were associated with war, and the positions of Venus were used as a timetable for fighting auspicious battles.

The Great North Platform also has an ancient ball court. It has unique acoustic properties—a whisper at one end of the 500-foot court can be clearly heard at the other end! The Maya king and his audience watched the ball games from the stone bleachers. Games were played to the death—a death by decapitation. However, the winning captain would lose his life, not the reverse! It was believed that the winner would go straight into the heaven world without having to endure the many steps it ordinarily took to achieve salvation. Other games, as indicated earlier, were played against enemies.

On the great platform is a structure called a tzompantli, meaning "skull rack." On the surface of the platform are racks of human skulls from Maya enemies, especially the warriors from the rival state of Calakmul. There are also stone reliefs depicting skeleton warriors and eagles eating human hearts. In the Maya civilization, the eagle represents the authority and unity of a divergent group of people.

On the Great North Platform is another platform dedicated to eagles and jaguars. In the Maya military forces, the "Eagle Knights" were archers who composed the vanguard of troops approaching the enemy. The "Jaguar Knights" were the elite fighting force that followed. They fought enemies with clubs tipped with obsidian knives, and they also fought in hand-to-hand combat. They wore armor covered with jaguar skin, and their helmets had carvings of jaguars.

The Central Group has a building called Las Monjas, or "The Nunnery." Scholars differ as to whether or not it was a palace for the founders of Chichen Itza, a priest's house, or a council chamber. El Caracol ("The Snail") is located to the north of Las Monjas and is a winding staircase that leads to a four-cornered tower overlooking the surrounding countryside. The Akab Dzib is to the east of El Caracol, and it is a building that contains a sculpture of a priest holding a jar. There are glyphs on the pot that have yet to be translated.

The Osario Group is a smaller version of El Castillo, but the temple atop this step pyramid lies alongside a natural cave replete with stalactites and stalagmites. The cavern contained a treasure trove of gold and jade. There were also human bones present, indicating that it was used for human sacrifice.

Maya Achievements

The Maya used a mathematical system based on the number twenty, known as the vigesimal system. It was perfected around the year 900 BCE and consisted of a series of dots and dashes. The dots stood for single numbers, and the dashes stood for the number five. For numbers one to nineteen, the numbers were written horizontally. For numbers above nineteen, the numbers were written vertically, in powers of twenty. Above the number 400, another vertical column would be added, and so on.

The Maya calendar had three different tallying systems: the Tzolkin, or "divine" calendar, the Haab', or civic calendar, and the Long Count calendar. The Tzolkin was based on a year of 260 days, as well as upon the period of human gestation or the agricultural cycles of maize production. The Haab' calendar was based upon a year of precisely 365.2420 days, which was more advanced than that of the 1582 Gregorian calendar and the Long Count calendar, which was based on the beginning date of August 11th, 3114 BCE, the mythical date assigned to creation. On the circular calendars that were carved out of stone, it reached its end in the year 2012. While popular opinion during the 20th century indicated that 2012 predicted the end of the earth, experts stated that the calendric cycle merely starts over again.

The Maya developed an astronomical system based on the movements of Venus, the sun and the moon, Jupiter, Mercury, and Mars. They used this system to help the people schedule their sowing and harvesting times. Once their written language was deciphered, researchers discovered that the Maya correctly identified many of the constellations and were even able to predict eclipses.

There were three civilizations in the ancient world that developed a sophisticated written language independently—Mesopotamia, China, and the Maya civilization. The earliest form of the Maya script dates back to the 3rd century BCE. When this civilization collapsed in the 16th century, its people could write everything that they could say. Initially, they used glyphs to write and later developed a very complex system combining glyphs and phonetic representations to help the reader pronounce the word, much like what is done today in the Latin languages. Some glyphs represented whole words in everyday use, like "jaguar," and others, called syllabograms, were the signs for syllables. In the 20th century, nearly all of the Maya script was translated, but it still eludes computer decipherment.

The Mysterious Collapse of the Maya Civilization

By the year 1000 CE, many of the city-states in the southern lowland areas were abandoned. The time of the collapse was evidenced by a lack of dated artifacts after that year, as well as evidence that no new buildings were erected. Much of the population seemed to have disappeared or migrated north toward Yucatan. Historians thus refer to the period between 900 to 1000 as the collapse of the Classic Maya civilization.

The city of Palenque virtually collapsed in the year 711 CE, and there are no artifacts associated with the city of Toniná after 909. The city-states of Topan, Tikal, and Calakmul simply disappeared. The rainforest villages and city centers in the lowlands were swallowed up by jungles. Early explorers sometimes came across very small agricultural communities tucked away in the forests in the southwestern areas around current-day Guatemala. Only Yucatan continued to survive as a polity, but it was very decentralized.

Researchers have indicated that some of the causes for the decline of the Maya during the Classic Period was due to intertribal warfare, the decline of trade, the spread of disease, starvation due to nutritional deficiency, drought caused by deforestation, soil erosion (despite their attempts to prevent it), and soil exhaustion.

The Maya in Yucatan survived beyond the mysterious collapse of the Classic Period. Migration from the inland areas drew the population toward the coastal areas, specifically the Yucatan Peninsula and today's Guatemala. In Yucatan, most of the people lived along the coast and in the vicinity of Chichen Itza, continuing their traditional religious and social customs. As their primary crop was maize and beans, the people needed some kind of protein source. The coast provided fish, clams, and other shellfish, which are all a good source of protein. Agriculture diminished, though, due to the various factors mentioned above, mainly deforestation and soil exhaustion.

It is still a mystery to this day as to why the ancient Maya abandoned their native land. There are about six million Maya living today, and a small segment live on the Yucatan Peninsula, while others live in Guatemala, other parts of Mexico, and Belize.

The Spanish Conquest

There was a large gap of time between the Maya collapse and the invasion of new peoples, for it was in the 14th century that European colonization began. Between 1345 and 1521, the Aztec Empire grew, and its people settled north and northwest of the Maya territory.

In 1524, Hernán Cortés sent out an expedition of his conquistadors southeast of the Yucatan Peninsula. The Spanish warriors, equipped with broadswords, lances, matchlocks, and light artillery, rushed in, shouting, "Receive your bearded guests, the armies of God!" The Maya were shocked by the force of these devilish warriors. Maya weapons were more primitive, as they used spears, bows and arrows, and stones, but they fought back furiously. The Maya technique of ambush was often effective, but Cortés was able to make gains southeast of Yucatan.

Cortés, who, it should be noted, was not the first European to encounter the Maya (Francisco Hernández de Córdoba in 1517 was), returned to Spain, and eventually, Francisco de Montejo was sent in to conquer the Yucatan Peninsula. In 1527, he controlled northeastern Yucatan, and in 1531, he conquered the city of Chichen Itza and founded a Spanish sister town just north of the temple areas.

The Spanish felt that the Maya were infidels, and they made tremendous missionary efforts across the Yucatan Peninsula but were met with great resistance. Little by little, the Spanish conquerors under Francisco de Montejo subdued the towns along the coast. The missionary efforts continued, and the Spanish military presence grew substantially. In 1545, upon the subjugation of the Maya city of Champoton and the conversion of the Maya princes to Christianity, the Maya of Yucatan eventually accepted Spanish rule.

It wasn't until 1697, when the Spaniards of Yucatan, under Governor Martín de Urzúa y Arizmendi, they conquered Nojpetén in today's Guatemala, that the last significant Maya area in Central America fell. The Maya gods retired into their stone carvings and faded into the pottery and paintings on the abandoned walls of their caves and temples. With them, the Maya civilization, too, melted into the dusty past. However, some of the remaining Maya still celebrate their heritage and demonstrate their ancient customs for tourists.

Chapter 3 – The Aztecs (1250–1521 CE)

The Lost Land of Aztlan

Aztlan was an island and a legend. Archeologists and historians have sought for Aztlan for many, many years, as it is believed to have been the ancestral home of the Aztec people. Searches span from current-day Utah in the United States to western Mexico. Researchers also often use language as a means of identifying ethnic groups. Nahuatl was the root language used around the year 600 BCE. There were many dialects of that language, which have helped establish the fact that the people who settled in northern and central Mexico were from related ethnic groups.

The myth indicates that the people were composed of seven tribes, who eventually settled near Aztlan. The legend is contradictory at times, with some saying that Aztlan was a paradise. Others state that tyrannical leaders ruled the people. According to their ancient text, the Aubin Codex, the great god Huitzilopochtli led the people from the seven tribes into a new land. In the year 1064 CE, the great migration began. One of the tribes called themselves the Azteca. Their deity led them into the Valley of Mexico, which lies at the approximate center of today's Mexico, arriving around the year 1250.

The Valley of Mexico

Volcanoes surround this area, and all except two were active in the 13th century. Erosion from those volcanic mountains created fertile soil dotted by saline lakes, creating a wealth of food sources. The valley had some shallow lakes, and those bodies of water were salty, briny, or brackish. Much of the water in the streams was alkaline; thus, drinking water was at a minimum.

The steeper mountains were heavily forested with pine and oak trees. Those trees were cut and used for lumber, and the charcoal created from burning wood was used as a source of heat and for cooking.

To the north and south of this central region, the conditions were different. The northern area was populated by different people, the Otomi, who spoke a different language than the Aztecs. Their territory was located in the plains, within today's state of Hidalgo. It was significantly drier, and the soil wasn't rich. There, they raised agave plants, using them as sources of fiber and syrup. It was, however, a good area to find obsidian, which was used for tools, weapons, and jewelry.

To the east and west of the Valley of Mexico lay the Puebla and Toluca Valleys. The soil there was fertile, suitable for the growing of edible crops. To the south lay the Valley of Morelos. This was the most fertile area. The hot wet climate was ideal for the cultivation of fruit, and cotton could also be grown within certain areas.

The Arrival of the Aztecs

When the Aztec people arrived in the Valley of Mexico, the area was already settled by indigenous tribes who had established some city-states—Chalco, Xochimilco, Tlacopan, Culhuacan, and Azcapotzalco. The people settled on the hillsides in the west of current-day Mexico City. However, the people of one of the city-states, Azcapotzalco, forcibly removed them from that area. Feeling compassion for them, Cocoxtli, the leader of the neighboring city-state of Culhuacan, gave them an area in which to live in 1299. It lay within his city-state and was called Tizaapan, although the Aztecs called it Chapultepec. In exchange for the grant of the land, the Aztecs often fought alongside the warriors of Culhuacan in their wars with other city-states. They also mingled with the people there, and some of their men married women from Culhuacan.

In 1323, the people asked for the daughter of Achicometl, the leader of Culhuacan, so they could make her a goddess, whom they wished to name Yaocihuatl. What the Aztecs failed to do was inform Achicometl that the process in which she would be deified entailed sacrificing her to Xipe Totec, one of their gods. This was considered a privilege and an honor to the Aztecs. Once they received her, they then sacrificed the young woman and flayed her. When the king of Culhuacan discovered this, he was furious and forced them to leave. The Aztecs then prayed to their god Huitzilopochtli, also known as the god of war, for direction.

The myth drawn on the walls and in the caves of this new land tells the story. Huitzilopochtli told the people to look for tall nopal cactuses with eagles atop them. There, he said, they were to build their capital city, Mexica-Tenochtitlan. According to the legend, the god said, "From where the eagles are resting, from where the tigers are exalted...Who shall conquer Mexica-Tenochtitlan? Who could shake the foundation of heaven?" Mexica-Tenochtitlan was an island city lying in Lake Texcoco in the Valley of Mexico and was located near today's Mexico City. It was founded in 1325 by the Aztecs.

Mexica-Tenochtitlan

Etymologically, the name of this island-city means "rock" and "prickly pear." It is situated toward one side of Lake Texcoco, which is very shallow, so mostly canoes were used as modes of transportation and for the shipment of supplies. The city centers were connected to the surrounding areas by causeways and bridges, and so, it became the center of trade and government as well. The bridges were moveable to defend the city against invaders, and the city itself was networked with canals.

Because of the high degree of salinity in the lakes in central Mexico and around Mexica-Tenochtitlan, people sought out fresh spring water. In the early 13th century, their early leader was called on to figure out this problem. Wisely, he engaged his people in building the Nezahualcoyotl levee, which redirected fresh water from an underground spring into the heart of the city. The brackish waters were then redirected to the east and controlled by a series of dikes. From the spring, another network of aqueducts was built to bring fresh water into the city. This welcome fresh water was used for cleaning, cooking, and bathing. It should be noted that these people were not only talented but also cleanly. They used two kinds of soap made from the roots of the Saponaria americana and the Agave americana plants. They even had sauna-like baths for their pregnant women.

The city had both functional and beautiful stone structures that lent to its magnificent beauty. Later explorers admired the skills of the Aztecs, and Bernal Díaz del Castillo, an early conquistador, said:

> When we saw so many cities and villages built in the water and other great towns on dry land, we were amazed and said that it was like the enchantments on account of the great towers and cues and buildings rising from the water, and all built of masonry. And some of our soldiers even asked whether the things that we saw were not a dream? I do not know how to describe it, seeing things as we did that had never been heard of or seen before, not even dreamed about.

Marketplaces were built in Tlatelolco, a sister city of Mexica-Tenochtitlan, which was founded for trade and commerce. Estimates of the number of people frequenting that area ranged between 20,000 to 40,000 people per day. The high numbers occurred on the dates of feast days and sacrificial ceremonies.

In Mexica-Tenochtitlan proper, public buildings were founded. Their main god, Huitzilopochtli, had a prominent temple called the Templo Mayor, which also paid respect to the all-important rain god Tlaloc. There was also a temple to their feathered serpent god, Quetzalcoatl.

In the city, there was a space devoted to their ritual ball game, which they called tlachtli, as well as and a tzompantli, a rack of skulls. The skulls were those of their enemies and were used to warn away other potential invaders.

The Triple Alliance

In 1376, they appointed Acamapichtli to be the first ruler of Mexica-Tenochtitlan. He was the product of the union of an Aztec woman and a man from Culhuacan. After Acamapichtli of Mexica-Tenochtitlan died, his son, Huitzilihuitl, became the new emperor, and he sought alliances among the small city-states to unite the country. In 1417, Chimalpopoca, Huitzilihuitl's son, was the next ruler, who was succeeded by Itzcoatl, one of Acamapichtli's sons in 1427.

The conflicts among the city-states continued until the year 1428, for it was this year that, under the leadership of Itzcoatl, Mexica-Tenochtitlan, Texcoco, and Tlacopan became allies. The coalition was somewhat tenuous. It was more or less an agreement to keep some semblance of peace among them. Each of the three city-states was strong in their own right, however.

Each city-state still had its own government, and a group of elders from each of the prominent city-states elected an emperor that would lead all three. The emperor resided in the central city-state of Mexica-Tenochtitlan. The emperor, though, didn't interfere in the administrations of the other two city-states but rather kept the area united. Itzcoatl was the emperor of the Aztecs after the formation of the Triple Alliance. His reign ended in 1440.

Inauguration of the Aztec Empire

The Triple Alliance conquered the adjoining city-states to its east and west until the Aztec territory spread from one shore of the Gulf of Mexico to the opposite coast of the Pacific Ocean. The city-states, or *altepetl*, were usually ruled by the hereditary elite. In the case of outlying conquered lands, the central administration in the capital maintained their control by establishing a puppet government or having a military force present. Each city-state paid tribute to the central government in Mexica-Tenochtitlan, and the common people were expected to make contributions. Tribute could be paid in the form of products, which could include agricultural products or goods such as beads, crafts, and even useful commodities such as lumber or tools.

During his reign, Itzcoatl united Mexica-Tenochtitlan with Texcoco and Tlacopan to expand the size of their holdings. They conquered Huexotla, Coatlinchan, and Tepoztlan, and they obtained titular control of Xochimilco, Culhuacan, and Mixquic. They divided these city-states amongst themselves and converted them into tributary states.

Moctezuma I, the successor of Itzcoatl in 1440, encountered rebellions from some of those tributary states and had to reconquer them. After being successful on those fronts, he conquered Xalapa, Cosamaloapan, Cotaxtla, and Ahuilizapan, and he also reconquered some of the lost segments of the rebellious Huexotla state.

Aztec Society

Acamapichtli, the first ruler of Mexica-Tenochtitlan, had many descendants, and he was essentially the father of the noble and priestly class, which was called *Pipiltin*. They were more educated than the rest of the population, but their jobs weren't always just one of leadership. Some were craftsmen, and others were involved in business.

The next lower class was the *macehualtin*, which consisted of farmers, tradesmen, warriors, and artisans. The artisans, in particular, were considered extremely important, as they were responsible for construction projects. Temples were considered the most important of their structures.

The class after the *macehualtin* was the *pochteca*. They were foreign tradesmen, many of whom resided in the country, who distributed, processed, and sold goods and wares. The Purepecha Empire, just northwest of the Aztecs, were one of their greatest trading partners, despite the fact that the Purepecha became involved in turf wars with the Aztecs for territorial dominance.

The lowest class was *tlacotin*, or the slaves. They were made up of captured people, debtors, and even criminals. Slaves could own possessions, and some also had slaves of their own. Slaves usually remained in their position indefinitely unless they could buy their way into freedom by paying their purchase price.

Economy and Agriculture

As with Mexica-Tenochtitlan, aqueducts were built through the land. For the farms, there was a system of irrigation and fertilization. On the slopes and in the higher elevations, terracing was typical.

Human waste was disposed of in a primitive sewage system, which broke it down for fertilizer. As most of their consumables were plant products and fish, their waste was biodegradable. Therefore, it could be used as an environmental-friendly fertilizer.

The people grew maize, herbs, fruit, squash, chilies, red peppers, and amaranth. For additional protein, they ate fish, insects, shrimp, and shellfish, as well as waterfowl. They didn't raise barnyard animals except for turkeys. After they expanded their territories south, they enjoyed fruits of all kinds.

They traded the excess foodstuffs that could be preserved, along with pottery, jewelry, and medicines made from herbal mixtures. Trading was usually conducted using the barter system.

Textiles

Ever since prehistorical times, the Aztecs had a hardy production of textiles, although the fabrics they used lacked variety. They utilized the fibers of agave plants, palm trees, and cotton from the hotter coastal regions. Cotton was reserved for the elites, and for more ornate dress wear for celebratory occasions, bark paper was used.

The Arts

The Aztecs traded colorful printed shawls and clothing, along with jewelry made from stones they had received from other trade deals. Ceremonial knives and generic face masks with feathers were also quite popular.

Turquoise was perhaps the most highly prized ornamental stone. It was used in the making of intricate mosaics and masks that were worn by the priests at their sacrificial ceremonies. The magnificent turquoise mask of Xiuhtecuhtli, whose name translates to "Turquoise Lord," is one such example. He represented the god of fire and heat. Quetzalcoatl, the feathered serpent, was often represented in artwork, as he was one of the most important deities, not only of the Aztecs but of the Olmecs and the Maya as well. In Mesoamerica, Quetzalcoatl became a creator god and the god of death and resurrection. As such, his image was a common theme in their sculptures and art.

Aztecs believed that the beauty of their art would serve to impress other cultures of their magnificence and power. Some of the Aztec treasures are currently in the prestigious British Museum.

Religion and Human Sacrifice

There were five creator gods of the Aztecs: 1) Huitzilopochtli, the god of war; 2) Xipe Totec, the "Flayed One"; 3) Quetzalcoatl, the feathered serpent; 4) Tezcatlipoca, the god of darkness; and 5) Ehecatl, the god of the wind. In their history, it says that "Huitzilopochtli is first in rank, no one, no one is like unto him...so daily do I send these praises coming forth in the garb of our ancestors: I shine; I glitter." Because wars were needed to create and expand the Aztec civilization, Huitzilopochtli was deemed the most important.

Whenever the sun set and the sky grew black, the Aztecs were deathly afraid that the sun wouldn't return. This belief can be seen in the people's attitude to the many wars, as the people were terrified that, come tomorrow, their civilization would end, destroyed by an evil and dark nation. They theorized that the setting of the sun meant that Huitzilopochtli fought against the darkness, and the darkness won, bringing death to the Aztecs. They needed the birth of the sun in the morning to keep living. The price for the sunrises would periodically be paid for in blood. Those who were sacrificed would rise to join Huitzilopochtli in battle, and, in return, a new day would be won.

Bloodletting was the most common form of sacrifice, which was usually done through the piercing of the tongue or a testicle. However, the Aztec calendar ran in cycles of eighteen months each, at the end of which a human sacrifice was necessary. Usually, the person was an enemy, or it could have been someone from one of their own city-states. The subjects were placed upon a slab in the temple, and their hearts were cut out of them. Then the heart was thrown down the temple stairs, and the gruesome task was done.

Other techniques were also used, such as hand-to-hand combat, death by arrows, drowning, and burning.

In the ancient Mesoamerican text, the Madrid Codex, it says:

> Awaken, already the sky is tinged with red,
>
> already the dawn has come,
>
> already the flame-colored pheasants are singing,
>
> the fire-colored swallows,
>
> already the butterflies are on the wing.
>
> For this reason, the ancient ones said,

he who has died, he becomes a god there,

which means that he died.

The Aztecs believed in an afterlife, but its nature depended upon the quality of life the person had lived. In the above lyric, two outcomes are mentioned—reincarnation as a bird or as a butterfly. Those who weren't victims of sacrifice had to wander as disembodied spirits within the slimy levels of the underworld, where it was not so brightly lit. Some would find their way to heaven, but those whose lives weren't meritorious might wander forever.

The Flower Wars

From 1454 to 1519, the city-states of Texcoco and Tlaxcala and the tributary states of Cholula and Huejotzingo intermittently endured drought and poor harvests, so they decided to stage ritual wars to satisfy the gods. Because they felt that the gods also needed periodic appeasement, they set places and dates at to where and when the combat would occur. Also, they didn't use their traditional weapons; instead, they used less-lethal weapons. Commoners and nobles both participated.

These wars, which began in 1454 and lasted until 1519, were also used to develop military prowess, much like the "war games" fought today by the military. Besides, it was an excellent way of demonstrating their powers to potential enemies, and city-states that lay outside of the boundaries of the Aztec Empire grew to greatly fear them.

These "wars" were called xochiyaoyotl wars, meaning "flower wars." A flower war was set up very much like a game because both sides had an equal number of warriors. The competitors in the flower wars were often city-states that had defied conquest by the Aztec Empire. Since past attempts to conquer these city-states ended in stalemates, partaking in a flower war would allow one to illustrate their strength and bravery on the battlefield. Oftentimes, the Aztecs used close-range weapons instead of their usual long-range ones. It would also allow each party to tend to the seeding and harvest, as well as provide a source for sacrifices.

Some of the outlying city-states harbored hostilities toward the Aztec Empire, such as Tlaxcala, Huejotzingo, and Cholula, and they were often challenged to combat chief members of the Triple Alliance and their loyal tributary states in a flower war. The goals of the flower wars were initially to capture prisoners, and it was understood that the land of the opposition would not be confiscated.

One of the unspoken goals of the flower wars was to weaken a potential opponent for actual conflicts. From another perspective, these flower wars were comparable to skirmishes, as it was a way for the Aztecs to learn about the strengths and weaknesses of their prospective enemies.

Empire Expansion

Under Emperor Ahuitzotl, the grandson of Itzcoatl, who gained control of the throne in 1486, the Aztec Empire made a considerable expansion. Although it was most likely an exaggeration, it was said that Ahuitzotl sacrificed more than 80,000 captives at the great temple of Tenochtitlan, the Templo Mayor. The empire was extremely wealthy due to all the tributes that poured in from the conquered lands. Ahuitzotl funded many building projects, one of which was a giant canal that brought water to the capital from Coyoacán. After the project was finished, the city flooded! The audacious priests unmercifully blamed the emperor, using as their excuse the rationale that the water goddess, Chalchiuhtlicue, was punishing the emperor for having stolen her water!

The Spanish Conquest of the Aztecs

In 1519, Hernán Cortés came into the Aztec Empire, first conquering the tributary provinces. He sent forth 400 vanguard warriors called the Totonac army, which was comprised of Mesoamericans that had allied with Cortés. At Tlaxcala, Xicotencatl the Younger attacked the Spanish. One of the Spanish conquistadors, Bernal Díaz del Castillo, described it as thus:

> As they approached us their squadrons were so numerous that the covered the whole plain, and they rushed on us like mad dogs, completely surrounding us, then they let fly many arrows, javelins, and stones, but with our muskets and crossbows and with good swordplay we did not fail as stout fighters...we fell upon the Indians with such energy that with us attacking on one side and the horsemen on the other, they soon turned tail.

What the people from Tlaxcala beheld were soldiers armed with muskets clad in shiny armor and sporting beards. The native people had never seen beards before, and it looked to them as if fur was growing from their faces. They had never seen horses before either, so when they saw each man on a horse, they thought it was one great beast.

Tlaxcala was one of the tributary provinces that often openly rebelled against Moctezuma II, who was a weak ruler, of which the Spanish took full advantage. Cortés met with the leader of Tlaxcala after the battle, and he told Cortés about his many grievances against Moctezuma. Cortés sympathized with him and convinced him that together they could defeat the emperor, and so, they formed an alliance.

Around 5,000 Tlaxcalans marched alongside the Totonac army and hundreds of regular Spanish soldiers. When they reached the capital city of Tenochtitlan, the Spanish troops were astonished. They saw large, highly decorated buildings, an intricate system of aqueducts, paved walkways, and arched overpasses. The city housed well over 100,000 inhabitants.

The Aztecs were awed by these new invaders and were afraid of their weaponry. They knew they were no match for them. In addition, after they looked upon the light-skinned face of Cortés, they felt he resembled their own deity, Quetzalcoatl—the powerful feathered serpent god. Moctezuma II welcomed them as if they were dignitaries, and he established relations with them and conducted six days of celebrations. Cortés and his allies took up residence in Tenochtitlan. Aware of the potential problems he might encounter in the future with the Aztec upper class, Cortés decided to round up the nobles and execute them during one of their ceremonies. He operated with reckless abandon, and since the Aztecs were terrified of his strength and power, they didn't openly resist.

Shortly thereafter, Cortés discovered that several Aztecs had killed some of his soldiers at Tlaxcala. In retaliation, he kidnapped Moctezuma II and held him. Cortés released him after a short period, but not long after that, Moctezuma was murdered. Historians differ on who was responsible, indicating that either some angry Aztecs did it because he permitted the city to fall to the Spaniards or that the Spanish did it. Upon the death of their emperor, the Aztecs behaved like a defeated people.

Cortes stayed in the area to administer it as its governor, but he was a poor administrator. He was in debt, and his lenders sued him. He left for Spain in 1540 and attempted to redeem himself by telling the emperor how many new land acquisitions were due to his efforts.

Relationship of the Aztecs and Their Spanish Overlords

The Spanish were fascinated by the art and architecture of the Aztecs, but that reaction was temporary. In time, they became appalled by their uncivilized practices and bloody religious rituals. To educate them in more acceptable conduct, at least according to European standards, Cortés assembled the leaders of the city and tried to convert them to Christianity. According to Bernal Díaz del Castillo, "Cortes explained the nature of our holy religion, and showed them the necessity of abolishing their idolatry and human sacrifices and other abominations." Over the years, scores of Christian missionaries would make it to the shores of the New World to spread Christianity to the peoples. Feeling that the European "gods" were more powerful than theirs, many converted.

There was some resistance in entirely surrendering their gods, so, for many years, many worshipped both their deities and the Christian god.

The arrival of the Spanish also brought the arrival of diseases, such as mumps, measles, and, worse of all, smallpox. The European soldiers had a built-up immunity to those diseases, so while some of the Spanish might have contracted smallpox, they had a greater resistance to it. As for the other illnesses, they weren't affected at all. However, the Aztecs died in huge numbers. A traveling missionary vividly described its tragic effects, "They died in heaps, like bedbugs. In many places it happened that everyone in a house died, and as it was impossible to bury the great number of dead, they pulled down the houses over them, so that their homes became their tombs."

To keep order, Cortés permitted the emperors to stay in power, although they had to attend to his orders. Thus, they allowed Moctezuma's heirs to continue to rule. Moctezuma's younger brother, Cuitláhuac, succeeded him. He organized a rebellion against the Spanish but lost. Although he was slightly successful during his rule, the great city of Tenochtitlan was in his hands for just a few months, for he died soon after taking over. It is thought that Cuitláhuac died of smallpox after ruling for only eighty days.

Cuitláhuac's cousin, Cuauhtémoc, assumed command of the Aztecs and reinitialized the revolt against the Spanish. Many of his soldiers fell ill with smallpox, and his forces had been depleted after the many battles against the Spanish. Nevertheless, these courageous warriors continued. However, against the firepower of the Spanish and the ravages of disease, they were helpless. Cuauhtémoc tried to escape but was captured and hanged. In the year 1521, the gleaming city of Tenochtitlan lay in ruins, and Mexico City, which was founded by Cortés, rose in its place.

Like Pigs

After the conquest, Cortés forced 8,000 people from Texcoco to dig a deep shipping channel to Tenochtitlan. He built a grand palace in the place of the markets and artisan shops in the city.

Cortés and his men were wide-eyed whenever they saw the beautiful gilded masks and jewelry the people wore. He ordered his men to collect all the gold they could find and bring it to him for distribution among the conquerors. The Mexicans of later generations said, "They hungered after gold like pigs."

The Glitter Died

In 1521, the Aztecs became a subservient people. They had lost their great and glittering island city of Tenochtitlan. They had long ago been told by their creator god, Huitzilopochtli, that a wondrous future awaited them when they ventured out of Aztlan, and although their civilization lasted for nearly four centuries, it was now gone. Their Spanish overlords forced them to dismantle their stone edifices and rebuild buildings after the strange style of Europe. To the Aztecs, Christianity was nothing more than stilted protocols and rituals. They believed, however, that the Spanish God must have been more powerful than their own gods. Despite this, the Aztecs still harbored little tables and makeshift altars to their old gods. Had their deities simply abandoned them? Were they just displeased? The Aztecs prayed to their gods but were only met with silence.

After Hernán Cortés mounted the siege of the great temple and the city of Tenochtitlan, all the Aztec idols were forcibly removed and replaced with Christian statuary. As stated above, Cortés had formed an alliance with the Tlaxcalans, and with their help, the sacred temples and altars were destroyed. The furiously persistent Aztecs even cut the still-beating hearts out of Spanish soldiers and burned them in sacrifice to their god, Huitzilopochtli. These rebellions continued to spring up for years after the initial conquest.

The land of the Aztecs was called New Spain, and it eventually became a part of Mexico, which was based on the ancient name given to the Aztecs by the gods: "Mexica."

Chapter 4 – The Andean Civilizations and the Incas

Norte Chico Culture (Caral-Supe Civilization) (3500– 1800 BCE)

On the western coast of South America in modern-day Peru, the indigenous tribes eked out a living on the steep slopes of the Andes Mountains. It remains a volcanic region to this day, and it is a part of the Ring of Fire, a popular name for the series of volcanoes that surround the Pacific Ocean. Theories project that its indigenous people migrated south from Mesoamerica, but some historians call the area a "cradle of civilization," which was just slightly after Mesopotamia and ancient Egypt. It even predated the Olmecs of Central America, who were there in 1500 BCE.

It was a mountainous area with many rain shadows, which is where rain falls on the windward side (or western side) of the mountains, and the leeward side has little to no rainfall. The leeward side of the craggy mountains was arid and nearly impossible to cultivate, while the windward side was subject to floods, runoffs, and consequential erosion.

Unlike other ancient societies, the people of Norte Chico had no pottery nor ceramics. They used cut-out gourds, which grew wild. On many of the fragments that have been found were circular and rectangular designs surrounding the wide-eyed faces of deities.

They built massive platform pyramids with a complexity of design that amazes historians. The bricks used for their construction were very different, as they weren't made of solid stone; they were instead made of tight netting stuffed with reeds and covered in stones. These structures show that their irrigation systems were remarkably intricate.

The fields were covered with cotton, much of which was used to make fish netting, clothing, and bags. These nets were exchanged for fish and other products, which were traded along a network of canals leading to the coast, and some trade was conducted with the inland tribes. Like Mesoamerica, maize was their staple crop.

There was no written language per se, but it is conjectured that these clever people composed words and phrases using knots. Their chief deity was the Wari-Tiwanaku, the Staff God. He was a fanged figure depicted with two staffs and entwined with snakes. He was the precursor of the Inca god of thunder, lightning, and rain.

Archeological evidence of the Norte Chico culture shows that their society diminished in 1800 BCE. The agricultural terraces that the people built were found farther north, indicating that the people most likely migrated there. It is thought that the soils had become less arable from the constant snowmelt that washed away all the soil's natural nutrients.

Chavín Culture (850 BCE– 200 BCE)

Chavín de Huantar is a notable architectural accomplishment in Peru, located 160 miles north of Lima. It served as a worship center, and it was constantly added to and reworked from generation to generation. The building is at the head of a sunken circular plaza used for sacrifices and ceremonies.

Like the Olmecs and the Maya of Central America, the population worshiped, among other gods, the jaguar. Archeologists have noted that the canals they built on the slope were of such a configuration that the wind raced through the channels, causing a sound like that of the roar of the jaguar.

Their great temple, called the temple complex of Chavín de Huantar, is a U-shaped stone structure of staircases, sculptured mounds, passages, and paved walkways. It's situated at an altitude of almost 10,500 feet and is, as one might expect, located in the Andes. Their creator god, also called Chavín de Huantar, was depicted as a humanoid figure with a feline head. Carvings show anthropomorphic figures blowing into giant conch shells called pututus. Researchers have discovered that they produced warbling sounds in the key of C major, and the sound is not unlike that of the trombone. Different notes are obtained by lip control.

Their shamans may have regularly ingested biochemical substances made from the San Pedro cactus, which trigger an altered state of consciousness. As mentioned above, the Chavín venerated the jaguar, and sculptures of jaguars were plentiful and incorporated into vases and drinking vessels.

It is said that the Chavín built temples and underground shelters for religious ceremonies. Human burial sites were unearthed by archeologists within these catacombs, although some researchers theorize that those were the remains of people who had built the temples. Others posit that those human remains could have come from the bodies of those who were sacrificed to the gods. Offerings to the deities consisted of ceramics, obsidian fragments, and conch shells. Worshippers would often smash pottery on the ground as offerings.

The Chavín people were peaceful, a factor that was common in harsh geological areas, as their efforts were expended in maintaining agriculture and the conservation and rationing of water resources.

They did not grow as much maize as the indigenous people that lived to the north because the rainfall was unpredictable. Instead, their basic crops were potatoes and quinoa. Freshwater clams were harvested in the mountain lakes, and deer and birds were hunted in the forested regions. Llamas were common on the high elevations and were domesticated for transportation and for use as pack animals.

In time, the land became overly domesticated and suffered from erosion, which was common at higher elevations. Trade also diminished, and as the neighboring communities increased in size, it has been theorized that warfare all but obliterated the Chavín.

The Chimú Culture (900 CE– 1470 CE)

The Chimú culture originally existed in the areas once occupied by the Moche people; thus, the history of those two groups was fused into what is called the "Chimú-Moche" or "Early Chimú." The Moche were possibly forced out due to an earthquake or drought. According to the ancient legends, however, the Moche people were defeated by the sons of Tacaynamo, Guacricaur, and Ñancempinco. Tacaynamo, the legend states, was born from a golden egg from the great sea and sailed with his fleet of balsa wood rafts. The land, under his wise rule and that of his nine descendants, expanded the "empire" 600 miles down the western coast of South America.

Their empire was peppered with citadels, which were elaborate open-air adobe structures composed of diamond-shaped windows, passageways, and ceremonial altars. The Kingdom of Chimor was the center of this empire, whose capital was Chan Chan.

The kingdom had a well-organized hierarchy, and the officials were in charge of the essential aspects of society, such as land and water use and distribution, labor, rural and city engineering, maintenance, crafts, and administration. The culture was wealthy and became the envy of bordering countries.

The kings and nobles would have been adorned in high-quality textiles made from camelid wool, which is much softer than sheep's wool. Gold and silver jewelry were sewn into their garments. The men sported decorative feathers imported from the "cloud forests" of the Andes Mountains and the Amazon rainforest, and the women wore elaborate necklaces of Spondylus shells. The Spondylus shells were also imported by the Chimú, which they got from current-day Ecuador. The Spondylus shells, when crushed, create a red tint, which was used to dye the carpet the king walked on in the city square.

To create these beautifully decorated textiles, the people used looms. Besides camelid wool, the people also used cotton. The dyes came from organic sources such as tannins, walnuts, or cochineals, which looks like a beetle but is more closely related to cicadas. The practice of crushing their bodies for the red dye it produced was not only used by the Chimú; Mesoamerican cultures, like the Maya and Aztecs, did this as well.

Their pots, which were made of clay, consisted of two bulbous containers with one spout. When the drink was poured, the pots whistled like today's teapots. Some of their pottery, called blackware, was created in a closed kiln where the clay object itself wasn't exposed to the air.

Their main crops, which favored the rich loamy soils, were guava, oranges, citrons, and figs. Scents of delicate varieties wafted in their cultivated gardens and included poinsettias, mimosas, bougainvillea, geraniums, and the night-blooming jasmine.

Their use of a canal system was highly advanced for the time, and historians have said that the people created arable fields in the desert. Fishermen traveled the seas in reed rafts called caballitos de totora, which translates to "little reed horses." They were made from the totora plant, which is large and long. The finished product resembles a canoe with a snubbed back. Some fishermen still use this style of boat today.

The Chimú developed a great respect for water conservation and built elaborate water management structures. Water became an object of worship, and they developed a water cult. Among their objects of worship were fountains and mountain streams. Some of the controlled waterfalls were fed by underground springs. The water, it is said, tasted like seltzer water. Stairways were built with miniature aqueduct-like structures that permitted the water to flow down the steps. The water goddess was called Ni. The Chimú showed a great reverence toward nature, shaping statues of the god of fish and the god of the seas in silver.

The Chimú also worshipped the moon, whom they called Shi. In Chan Chan, they erected a temple to this goddess. Their leader, the Grand Chimú, would enter the temple wearing a diadem of jewels and a robe with a mosaic woven on it, featuring bird feathers. Flowers of the passion fruit overhung the walkway where he would make his grand entrance.

In 2012, archeologists unearthed the burial site of 140 children in Huanchaco, just north of Chan Chan. Tragically, they had been sacrificed, along with numerous camelids. The children had decorative hats on and were buried facing the sea, while the camelids that were buried faced the Andes. The researchers felt that they were given *chicha*, corn beer, to tranquilize them before the priests thrust great swords into and across their sternums. Quite possibly, their hearts were dug out and burnt in metallic containers before the gods. Because of the geological evidence of a layer of heavy dried mud, within which the children were buried, archeologists surmise that the sacrifice was meant to make a tribute to the gods to prevent the continued effects of El Niño sometime during the years of 1400 to 1450.

In the small protruding peninsula of Paracas, elongated skulls were unearthed. This elongation came about as a result of the practice of head binding, which started when individuals were just children. In some cultures, people did this as a sign of beauty. It appears that the Chimú did this as a status symbol, as they are most often found in the family tombs of the high priests and royals.

In 1471, the Chimú were conquered by the very powerful Incas under Túpac Inca Yupanqui. The Incas surprised them by coming into their lands from the north rather than the south. They captured Minchancaman, the Chimú emperor, and led him out of Chan Chan, after which the Incas took over the city.

The Incas did permit the Chimú people to have some degree of autonomy, which lasted until the year 1532.

The Incas (1438– 1533 CE)

Towering over 3,000 feet in the air at the hilltop is the citadel-shaped peak of Sacsayhuaman. Below it was the puma-shaped city of today's Cusco in Peru. This was "the navel of the world," over which the power of the spirits would reign. From the elegant peak ran the River Tullumayo. It was the task of Manco Capac, the founder of the Inca Empire, to find it. And so, he did.

Manco Capac, according to one legend, emerged from a watery cave in Lake Titicaca along with his brothers, Ayar Auca, Ayar Cachi, and Ayar Uchu, as well as his four sisters. In a variation of the legend, Manco Capac was the son of the creator god Inti. The legend states that Manco Capac's brothers turned to stone, which often happened in the mythology of the day.

Manco Capac came from a nomadic tribe. He and his followers traversed the Andes Mountains in search of new land for the people. As they descended the craggy slopes of the formidable Andes, they were encountered by several small tribes of indigenous peoples: the Sahuares, the Alcahuisas, and the more numerous Huallas. After they settled in the valley city of Cusco, they often encountered fierce tribes from neighboring regions. However, the Inca were skilled hunters and fighters, having spent many years developing their armor and weaponry. They used bronze-tipped spears, arrows, darts, axes, wooden slings, and two-edged swords with serrated blades, the latter being used with great alacrity. Their armor was less secure in a sense, as it hung loosely about their bodies, making rapid, unexpected movements possible. After all, swift motion is essential in hand-to-hand combat. Boys joined the military, which was voluntary, when they were young, and they grew up exercising their skills.

The ancient name of the Inca land was Tawantinsuyu, and they spoke a language known as Quechua. It is believed that many of the indigenous tribes of the western coastal regions of South America, like the Norte Chico and Moche, spoke dialects related to that language, as they were similar to the language of the Incas.

Manco Capac became the first king of Cusco, and he reigned from 1150 to 1178. According to Inca beliefs, after he died, his body turned to stone. One of the most illustrious Inca emperors was Pachacuti Inca Yupanqui, the ninth ruler of the Incas. His reign began in 1430, and during it, he managed to establish the Inca Empire as a force to be reckoned with. His name appropriately means "earth-shaker." He and his valiant son, Túpac Inca, carved out a city center and created a place for the Inca people to flourish.

These rulers were wise and messaged the neighboring tribes, saying that they wanted to join with them to create a viable empire. The Incas had a wealth of textiles to offer as gifts and promised the other tribes they would be wealthy. Those tribes that cohabited the region realized that these Incas were powerful and accepted their rule. It was unwise not to do so because the military superiority of the Inca was well known. Although most of the tribes were cooperative, some weren't, namely the Chanka and the Chimú.

The highlands of Peru, located north of Cusco, was inhabited by the Hanan Chankas. Their warfare was bloody, as were the punishments of their conquered people. Sometimes, they flayed them slowly by cutting the skin around the toes and peeling it off, sadistically relishing the captive's screams. In 1430, the Chankas descended from the high plateaus and attacked the Inca in their growing city of Cusco. Pachacuti and Túpac raced in with their highly trained troops of hardened Inca warriors to stop them.

In 1438, the Inca handily defeated the Chankas at the bloody Battle of Yawarpampa. Before the great battle, Pachacuti prayed to the gods. According to a legend, stones were converted into fighting men, who helped Pachacuti and Túpac wipe out the enemy before returning back to their stone form. Historians, however, believe that some fighters from their allied tribes came to their aid and that the legend was a way to grant themselves mystical powers. After the conflict, the leaders of the Chankas were executed, and their children were trained in the ways of the Incas. Their lands were confiscated, and the empire expanded to control nearly all of today's Peru.

Machu Picchu

The illustrious Pachacuti ordered the construction of the world-renowned site of Machu Picchu in the year 1450. Originally built as a palace, it became a veritable community. The city of Machu Picchu rises to a height of around 8,000 feet above sea level, and the iconic mountain seen in photos of the ancient city is Huayna Picchu. The natural structure of Machu Picchu consists of a series of crags and cliffs that reach to and even above the clouds. Within one of the cliffs is a secret entrance to a military garrison, which was hidden deep within the caverns.

The valley between the two mountain peaks, created by the intimidating Urubamba River that flows past them, is shaped like a saddle. Since the ground is very fertile due to the wondrous mountain springs, Machu Picchu was terraced.

The Temple of the Sun is its crowning achievement. In typical Inca style, the structure is made of stone using ashlar masonry. Ashlar isn't simply a type of stone; it is stone that has been so meticulously cut that each stone fits together perfectly. No mortar is needed. There are low reliefs carved into the stone representing gods and aspects of everyday Inca life. The temple is built in a semicircular fashion and has a lower level leading to a series of pools.

Huge stone storage containers are there, which were used for grain and other food staples. A narrow window sits at one end and would have provided a breathtaking view of the summer solstice in the 15th century.

The great Intihuatana is another notable aspect of Machu Picchu. The Intihuatana is a sacred ritual stone that astronomers have conjected served as a clock and calendar. Its name is derived from Inti, who was their head god. The Incas believed that this rock held the sun in position as it moved along its path.

The peaks of Machu Picchu are riddled with caves, and Inti Mach'ay is one of them. It was used for the great festival of the sun and for the initiation of young nobles into manhood, whose test consisted of being subjected to an ear-piercing ritual. The cave is configured in a fascinating way. A tunnel-shaped window lets in sunlight only during the days around the winter solstice, after which the days become longer, and the cave goes dark for another year.

The Temple of the Condor at Machu Picchu is spectacular. It was as if nature itself knew what its sculptor wanted—a giant representation of the Andean condor, a large bird with an immense wingspan. In fact, it's the largest flying bird in the world. Beneath the stones that form the wings is a small cave housing a few mummies, the remains of prisoners who were sacrificed in honor of the condor, who was considered a minor god.

Machu Picchu was not the only architectural achievement of the Incas. Although less impressive, Huánuco Pampa was an Inca city that lay on a flat grassland that extended along a north-south segment just inside the western coast. It is situated on a high plateau rising nearly 12,000 feet above sea level.

The grass of the Peruvian plains is called ichu grass, and since it is stiff and straw-like, it was used to construct houses and stiffen adobe bricks. As many as 30,000 people inhabited the long narrow plateau, living a mostly agrarian life. Many of the buildings were unfinished, which tended to happen during the waning days of the empire. Plans and conquests in the interest of expansion outpaced the empire's ability to build up their cities and towns.

In the center of Huánuco Pampa lay a huge flat ceremonial platform. From this platform, the nobles would reenact historical events ritualistically. It was also used as a place for grand military rallies.

Portions of the city were dedicated to the shops of craftsmen and women, like pottery makers and textile weavers, as well as plazas for socializing, buying, and selling. There were smaller structures for the town dwellers, farmers, and tradesmen, but there were several larger residences built of red stone that were for the royalty and the emperors whenever they traveled through this land. The structures seen there resemble the kinds observed in Cusco.

Like many other cultures before them, the Incas had an organized means of food conservation. Outside of its most populous city of Cusco, the Incas wisely had storage facilities, which were prevalent in Huánuco Pampa. These were food towers called *colcas*, which were erected on the hillsides and contained grains, maize, lima beans, potatoes, and the like.

Huánuco Pampa might have needed these towers more than other cities, as it was bisected by a 15,000-mile north-south path, simply called the "Inca Road." This road provided transportation to and from the far-flung areas of the north to those in the south. It was essentially the "spine" of the Andes. Goods were mostly transported on llamas and consisted of spectacularly colored bird feathers, salt, precious stones, and shells. The road was interspersed with descending flagstone steps and earthen causeways across gorges.

In 1572, the Spanish invasion disrupted the growth of the Inca civilization. Up until that point, Huánuco Pampa was the center of commerce. Luis Felipe Mejo, one of the leading archeologists of the Incas, said that "It was a major site that crashed, and nothing replaced it."

Expansion of the Incan Empire

In 1471, Túpac Inca succeeded his father, Pachacuti. His father had looked toward conquering the entire western coast of current-day Peru, and so, Túpac decided to carry on that dream. This was the land of the Chimú people, who had been there since 900 CE. By the time of Túpac Inca, the land was a fertile agricultural zone with an advanced irrigation system. Fisherman worked off the shores and brought in much protein-rich fish and shellfish. As mentioned above, Túpac conquered these people with his heavily armored forces, surprising them by attacking from the north instead of from the south. Part of the Chimú territory was in today's Peru, but another segment was in southwestern Ecuador.

Due to Pachacuti's and Túpac's efforts, they managed to expand the Inca Empire. It even stretched southward to the land of the Aymara people, who dwelled in the Andes Mountains. They lived in current-day southern Peru and western Bolivia, and the expansion into this territory was continued by Túpac's son, Huayna Capac. The Aymara were relatively independent people, only nominally operating under the auspices of the Incas.

The Inca Empire expanded southward but could only go so far as current-day central Chile, at the border of the Maule River, which intersects Chile horizontally. The indigenous people there, the Araucanians, were a mixture of nomadic tribes who lived in scattered villages. The Mapuche people also lived in this region, below the Maule River. Geneticists indicate that they came from a different bloodline than the Araucanians, and some ethnologists theorize they descended from mixed groups that initially came from Siberia, the Aleutian Islands, and, surprisingly enough, the Pacific Islands. Some are ethnically affiliated with the very first inhabitants of Japan, the Ainu. The Mapuche were never conquered by the Incas. After successfully battling the Incas, the Mapuche settled in today's regions of southern Chile, western Argentina, and the southernmost South American territory called Patagonia.

During the reign of Huayna Capac, who took the throne in 1493, the only tribe from the rainforest regions to resist the attack of the Incas was the Shuar. The Shuar were the fiercest of the tribes in the foothills of the Andes. Their warriors, it was said, operated like "fingers on a fist." According to the records, the people united against any invaders, saying that "the forest has always given us everything we need, and we are planning to defend it, as our ancestors would with the strength of a spear."

The Incas marched east, into the basin of the great Amazon River, to take on the Shuar. Defeating them would put the Incas in control of the lands they hadn't yet conquered in current-day Ecuador, and they planned on expanding that to small sections of today's Argentina and Colombia.

The region in which the Shuar lived was called the "Condor," and it was networked with many rivers, both large and small. Water pulsed through the Condor with a godlike roar as it made its way to the sea, and within the Condor were enormous caches of gold. The Incas wanted that gold, so the Shuar used whatever method they could to repel the would-be exploiters. The Condor was their home, and it was home to dozens of species of plants and wildlife never before seen by outsiders. For instance, the Incas had never seen a sloth hanging upside-down in a tree, and it was described by the European explorers as an uncouth animal, "which has great heaviness and slowness of movement and is called the PERICO LIGERO. He has the face of a monkey, has a shrill cry, climbs trees and eats ants."

The Shuar were known for their ability to create shrunken heads (*tsantsas*) from their decapitated enemies. They believed this would allow them to steal the spirits of their enemies and give them double the strength. They repelled the Incas in 1527, and to avoid being led away in captivity, the Incas gave them many gifts.

In the meantime, small groups of Spanish conquistadors were infiltrating Inca lands and had already taken the town of Tumbes, just south of today's Ecuador, in 1531. Some of these men came south from Central America, bringing diseases that were extremely lethal to the Incas, like smallpox. Emperor Huayna Capac died in 1524, and it is believed he died of smallpox. And he was not the only prominent Inca to so do, for his son and heir apparent, Ninan Cuyochi, also died of the disease. The nobles then selected the next son in line, Huascar, as the new ruler. However, a war broke out between him and his younger brother, Atahualpa. Huascar succeeded in conquering Atahualpa and his armies and imprisoned them. However, Atahualpa escaped and then moved upon his brother in what is known as the Battle of Quipanpan. In 1532, he was successful in overcoming his brother's troops, mostly due to an intervention from the Spanish conquistadors, who had been steadily moving into the Inca lands from Central America, which they had already conquered.

During that same year, the Spanish conquistador Pedro Pizarro invited Inca Emperor Atahualpa to meet with him in the city of Cajamarca. Atahualpa arrived on his litter in a procession of courtesans in royal robes. The emperor was quite drunk and was quite belligerent to the Dominican priest who approached him. In a loud voice, the emperor demanded that Pizarro return any lands he had confiscated on his way inland. Then the emperor noted the book the messenger was carrying and demanded it as well. It was a breviary, that is, a book of ritual prayers recited by Roman Catholic priests. After the priest handed it to Atahualpa, the emperor irreverently threw it on the ground. Immediately after that, Pizarro's soldiers, who had been hiding inside of the buildings, leaped out and killed nearly all of the Incas. Atahualpa was taken as a prisoner.

In November 1532, the Spanish invaders attacked the Incan army, handily won, and hauled off silver, gold, emeralds, and all sorts of precious metals. Not willing to give up easy, more Inca warriors amassed for an attack. They outnumbered the Spanish so badly that Pizarro decided to execute their leader. Pizarro placed Atahualpa on trial, although it was very much for show, and found Atahualpa guilty of idolatry and for the murder of his brother. Atahualpa was sentenced to die, and Pizarro planned to burn the emperor at the stake.

However, Atahualpa was extremely alarmed at this because the Incas believed that they would not be able to move on to the afterlife if their bodies were burned. The Dominican priest from the altercation before told Atahualpa that he would be able to change the nature of the sentence if he converted to Catholicism. Atahualpa consented. In the year 1533, he submitted himself to baptism and was later executed by strangulation.

The greatest calamity to hit the Incas wasn't the death of the emperor, though. It was all of the deaths by disease. With the Europeans came smallpox, and while some Europeans had survived the disease, the Incas hadn't built up any immunities to it. In just one district of the enormous Huánuco Pampa, an Inca told the chronicler Diego Ortiz de Zúñiga that the population of 4,000 dwindled to only 800. The great Inca land was now no more than a vassal state, and all the people were expected to pay tributes. Everyone was put to work regardless of age or class.

By 1541, even the Spanish had abandoned the plateau and established their new city, Huánuco, which was nearer the sea. Stones covered with dead grass aimlessly lie in the once-great plains of plenty. They stand like weathered tombstones, casting shadows over what was once the magnificent Inca Empire.

Chapter 5 – South America: Peru, Chile, Brazil, and Venezuela from Pre-Columbian Times through Colonization

Governmental Divisions

Between the 16th and the 20th century, Central and South America were divided into segments. South America is the main focus of the chapter, but information is included about Central America to give the reader a better understanding of how much power Spain, in particular, held.

The New Kingdom of Granada, which was formed in 1538 by the Spanish, oversaw northern South America and eventually became the Viceroyalty of New Granada in 1717. This included Venezuela, Colombia, and Ecuador, and it later stretched out to include Guyana, parts of Suriname, and the northern segments of Brazil.

And Spain didn't stop there. The Viceroyalty of Peru was formed in 1542 and ruled until 1824. The Viceroyalty of the Río de la Plata was established later than other viceroyalties, in 1776, and it covered the present-day territories in the Plate River Basin, including

Argentina, Buenos Aires, Bolivia, Paraguay, and Uruguay. Chile became a part of that viceroyalty in 1776 but had originally been a section of the Viceroyalty of Peru.

Spain's influence reached into Central America as well with the Viceroyalty of New Spain, which was originally created as a kingdom in 1521. Central America as far south as Costa Rica was a part of New Spain. However, the Spanish claims were grandiose. The Spaniards claimed that they possessed the North American states of New Mexico, Texas, Arizona, Colorado, Utah, Florida, and Louisiana under the Viceroyalty of New Spain. These huge territories were separated into large provinces, each with its own governmental bodies. New Spain lasted until 1821, the year Mexico won its independence.

As one can see, Spain was the dominant player on the field. The Portuguese did hold the Viceroyalty of Brazil, often referred to as the State of Brazil, but even they could not contend with the Spanish grab for power and wealth.

Cabildos

Cabildos were town councils that took care of local affairs. There was a judicial division, as well as the usual assortment of local officials, who oversaw the laws, clerical affairs, and taxes, which were similar to tributes paid to Spain by the various municipalities and cities. Local taxes were also charged.

Social Structure of South America under the Spanish

Social class was determined by one's heritage. The Spaniards who came over to South America via ships were considered members of the upper class. Those in the second group were called Criollos. They were of Spanish blood but were born in South America. These people were mostly landowners and wealthy merchants. The third group, called mestizos, were people of mixed blood. The next lowest class consisted of the indigenous peoples, and the lowest were the African slaves.

All economic efforts, including wealth and goods, went primarily to the support of New Spain. The administration spent a lot of its resources on defense to protect the country against invasions and native tribal raids.

The concentration of respect and money was held in the hands of the Spanish-born people, so the top-heavy concentration of wealth was a recipe for disaster.

Colonization of Peru

The Spaniards under Francisco Pizarro annexed the lands of the Incas in 1533. After the death of the last great Incan emperor, Huayna Capac, in 1524, Pizarro had permitted his sons, Atahualpa and Huascar, to share power. The heirs then engaged in a civil war, of which Atahualpa was the victor.

Weary of this conflict among the people of their conquered state, Pizarro staged a coup d'état. Following Atahualpa's death in 1533, the Spanish took over the main capital of Cusco. As expected, the Incas rebelled. One by one, these revolts were suppressed.

To make matters worse, a civil war broke out in 1541 between two competing conquistadors, Pizarro and Diego de Almagro II. Almagro was defeated and later executed. After this, there was a series of administrators, who usually only held the post until they were assassinated.

Since the European diseases severely reduced the native Incan population from twelve million to slightly more than one million, it was much easier for the Spanish to organize the governmental structure of Peru. In 1542, Spain created the Viceroyalty of Peru. Initially, it was a huge area encompassing the modern-day countries of Peru, Brazil, sections of Panama, Bolivia, Paraguay, Uruguay, Argentina, and other smaller countries. Since it was so very large, this territory was subdivided later on in 1717 with the creation of the Viceroyalty of New Granada, which encompassed Colombia, Ecuador, and Panama. In 1776, the newly-established Viceroyalty of the Río de la Plata included today's countries of Argentina, Bolivia, Paraguay, and Uruguay.

Pizarro founded the city of Lima in 1535, and it became the administrative center of the Viceroyalty of Peru and later on became its capital city. Because of the precious metals found in Peru, it became the wealthiest sector of South America. However, the Spaniards installed a program of forced labor using the native population.

There were mines sprinkled all over the area. Silver mines riddled Potosí, which is in modern-day Bolivia. Peru yielded gold, zinc, lead, tin, and other metals. Many of these ores and metals were shipped to Panama in Central America and then taken by ship to Seville, Spain.

In 1742, the Incan natives rebelled in the jungle areas. They despised many of the pureblood Spanish, the mestizos, and even the blacks. The natives were led by Juan Santos Atahualpa, who claimed to be descended from the Incan emperor Atahualpa. The rebels conquered a highland region but were then forced to retreat to the lowlands. That area was then placed in the hands of military governors, who kept the native population confined.

Another revolution occurred in 1780 under the charismatic leadership of Túpac Amaru II. The indigenous population and mestizos had been suffering under the lordship of the Spanish for several decades now, and it was as if a match was lit when Spain raised the sales tax on popular goods in 1778. The rebel forces conquered some provinces and expelled the royalist overlords. However, Amaru was killed in battle in 1781. Surprisingly, the rebellion did not collapse; in fact, it lasted for another year, and even after it was put down, small uprisings still occurred. It seemed as if the spirit of independence had been strengthened.

A new viceroy, José Fernando de Abascal y Sousa, came into power as the viceroy of Peru in 1806. Although he instituted educational reforms, he squashed all the revolts and riots. He reincorporated six provinces, including Chile and Quito (Ecuador).

Then he defeated the patriotic armies of the Argentinians. This did not quell the independence movement, though, as it continued to grow.

Chile

Diego de Almagro II, Francisco Pizarro's conquistador companion and sometimes rival, explored the land of the Incas in 1532 with Pizarro and annexed it in the name of Spain by the following year. In 1535, the two competitors openly warred over the control of the capital city of Cusco, Peru. Pizarro and his army of conquistadors were victorious in this struggle, so Pizarro moved into the Incan territories that later became Peru.

Diego de Almagro, on the other hand, traveled south and entered central Chile. He and his hardy men crossed the formidable Andes Mountains. The treacherous climb over the sharp crags and the frigid cold resulted in the loss of lives.

Upon reaching the valley near the Ñuble and Itata Rivers, he and his troops encountered the Mapuche. As mentioned above, when the Incas were in power, they were never able to subdue the Mapuche, who were very strong yet hostile. After meeting the Mapuche, Diego de Almagro and his fellow explorers retreated to the north.

Upon de Almagro's failure, Pizarro ordered Pedro de Valdivia to conquer Chile. Like de Almagro, Valdivia had conflicts with the Mapuche. Despite their presence, however, Valdivia managed to establish Spanish settlements, including the city of Santiago de la Nueva Extremadura (today's Santiago, Chile's capital). They permitted the Mapuche to keep their villages and settled in areas apart from them. Regardless, the Spanish were subject to many raids from the Mapuche. The conflicts between the Mapuche went on for 350 years, according to historians, but were sporadic in nature.

As more and more Spanish moved in, the Mapuche migrated farther south and intermarried with other indigenous tribes. They expanded their migration, eventually settling not only in Chile but Argentina as well.

Pedro de Valdivia became the governor of the newly established Captaincy of Chile in 1541. One of his earliest mandates was the division of labor among the people according to social status. He was on the hunt for the precious minerals that were nearly as common in this region than in Peru.

In 1544, he founded the city of La Serena in southern Chile and appointed Juan Bohón to administer over it. Once there, Bohón and his men encountered the notorious Mapuche, who rejected the forced servitude the Spanish placed upon them, setting off the Arauco War.

Arauco War

The conflict between the Spanish and the Mapuche lasted a very long time, beginning around 1560 and ending in 1662. There were many minor battles and skirmishes, with both sides pillaging, abducting and raping women, and seizing slaves, among other terrible acts. The Spanish were initially successful, but things took a turn during the Battle of Curalaba in 1598 when the Mapuche defeated the Spanish, and they followed up this success with the Destruction of the Seven Cities, an event in which the Mapuche destroyed or caused the Spanish to flee seven important outposts located south of the Biobío River. Many consider this to be the marker that signifies the beginning of the colonial period, for it was after this event that clear borders were made between Spanish and Mapuche lands.

In order to bring a workable peace between the warring factions, many meetings were held between the two. The resolution was a truce of a sort, with the Spanish holding land between the Biobío and Itata Rivers. This remained in place until Chile moved toward independence.

Brazil

Along the hot and steamy Amazon River in South America, between the years 1400 to 800 BCE, evidence of an early pre-Columbian civilization emerged. Although these were primitive times, complex societies did arise and flourish. Migrants trudged across Beringia, the land bridge connecting eastern Asia and North America. Some were also refugees from the warring tribes of Peru, Ecuador, and other societies of the Andes. Archeologists have conjectured that the early inhabitants who settled along the Amazon had impressive populations. They were called the Amerindians.

Two of the more prominent cultures of the Amazon region was that of the Marajoara and the Tupiniquim. It was determined that they originated in the Andes and fled to the Amazon, settling on island areas along the eastern coast. They were agrarians for the most part but did hunt and fish. They organized themselves into chiefdoms, but it is not known how their society was structured. Shamanism was their primary religious practice, and they also had various forms of ancestor worship.

The Mounds

In clearings, these indigenous people constructed great mounds. They left no written records, but archeologists have found funeral urns buried in the slopes of these structures. The urns contained only skeletal remains, and it is thought that the flesh was discarded after death. Along with the remains were ceramics, usually made of a clay-mud constituency. Its designs were geometrically-based. Some researchers have concluded that the mounds were used for defensive purposes. From the forensic evidence we have, it is thought that these people were strong, and it has been concluded that warfare among tribes often occurred.

Botanical studies have shown that there were attempts to control and manage growth. Some mounds appear to have been strategically placed and may have been used for flood control.

Crops

The soil in the Amazon region naturally welcomes the farmer, as it is black or nearly black due to the presence of huge quantities of organically decomposed materials and charcoal, not to mention a wealth of elements—nitrogen, phosphorus, and calcium—that give rise to life. This rivals the ingredients of commercially-produced potting soil. The Amazon variety is called terra preta. Unfortunately, the richness of the soil depletes rapidly in the presence of heavy forests, as the trees tend to absorb most of the best soil properties. The less-rich soils are called terra commun. They are rich in clay and support certain crops like sugarcane, rubber trees, coffee plants, and palm oil.

The Amazonian people cultivated cassava (also called manioc), which is a root crop. It was chopped and cooked to become a starch like tapioca. In addition to this, maize, beans, squash, and cotton were also raised.

Cannibalism

Cannibalism was practiced among most of the indigenous tribes of the Amazon Basin. It was believed that if one was to consume the flesh of a warrior, the deceased warrior's strength would be given to them. To guard against weakness, a warrior from one's own tribe was occasionally sacrificed and consumed. It was also considered by some to be a way of honoring them.

Portuguese Colonization of Brazil 1494– 1815

In 1494, the Treaty of Tordesillas was signed. It was decided by the great kingdoms of Portugal and Spain that they had inalienable rights to the newly discovered continents of North and South America. They also decided that not only should the Americas be divided between them but also the whole world. The treaty essentially drew a north-south line—the Tordesillas Meridian—halfway between the Cape Verde Islands and the current-day islands of Cuba and Hispaniola. All the land that lay to the east of that line was designated as belonging to Portugal, and all that lying to the west would be the property of Spain. Keep in mind that this was in 1494—territories like Mexico and Brazil had not yet been discovered. According to the treaty, which no other European country recognized, whichever country discovered new lands could keep those lands, meaning they could cross the line.

In 1500, Pedro Álvares Cabral explored the northeastern coast of South America. He has been credited as the discoverer of Brazil, which he claimed for Portugal. Pêro Vaz de Caminha, an early medieval writer, described the people of Brazil, saying, "They are brown-skinned, of a quite reddish complexion, with handsome faces and noses, nicely shaped. They go about naked, without any type of covering...They only eat yam [manioc or cassava] which is very plentiful here, and those seeds and fruits that the earth and the trees give of themselves."

Cabral's ambassador, Nicolau Coelho, made contact with the Tupiniquim. He left trinkets as gifts and celebrated a Roman Catholic mass. They also erected a cross to claim their findings. He then had his men chop down some brazilwood trees and took the logs back to Portugal. Not much time was spent in Brazil until 1530, as most of the foreign interest lay in trading with India.

The Brazilwood Rush

Once the ambassador for Pedro Álvarez Cabral brought back samples of brazilwood to Portugal, and its properties were discovered, the rush began. The Portuguese wanted to harvest it for the red dye that could be produced upon heating it, as it was quite valuable. Red connoted power, and thus, the elites relished it. They began enslaving the indigenous tribes, like the Tupinambá, to chop down the trees and haul it to their ships. The Portuguese were astonished at the strength of the tribesmen and continued to use them in other projects.

Once the brazilwood was marketed across Europe, word spread. The business became so lucrative for the Portuguese that they even set up factories. However, it also brought competition. Soon, French vessels arrived farther down the coast. They encamped there and harvested many trees. In 1530, the Portuguese sent Martin Afonso de Sousa to rid the area of the French.

Sugar Plantations

South America also became a new land in which sugar could be grown. The Portuguese were not only growing but also refining sugar because the value of the commodity was on the rise. It was dubbed "white gold," and it replaced honey, which was traditionally used in coffee. Mills were erected along the Atlantic coast of Brazil, and the current city of São Vicente and the state of Pernambuco in eastern Brazil were the most prosperous regions.

From 1534 onward, this industry took hold, and King John III of Portugal established a system of captaincies to control the country. Fifteen captaincies were distributed to the lower class of Portuguese noblemen, as well as sailors and merchants. These men bore the title of captains or *donatário*, and they provided for the administrations of their respective territory. Many of them failed, however, due to rivalries and insurgencies. Each captaincy answered to the overarching Governate General of Brazil, as well as the Crown of Portugal. This government body lasted on and off from 1549 to 1621. For brief periods of time, the Governate General was broken into two: the Governate General of Bahia in the north and the Governate General of Rio de Janeiro in the south.

Other European powers vied for a portion of profits from the sugar industry. The French gained hold for a short period in the early 17th century, followed by the Dutch. However, sugar was also grown in the Caribbean. Although Brazil remained the major exporter of sugar, competition from plantations in the Caribbean, especially Cuba, affected the market.

The presence of this industry was one of the most influential factors in the colonization of the Americas and the growth of the New World.

Insurrections

With the increase of European colonization came two predicaments: the increase of diseases among the Amerindians and slavery. Originally, the colonists enslaved the indigenous people to work on the sugar plantations. However, many caught the diseases the Europeans had carried over there, so the colonists switched to using mostly African slaves.

The resistance to slavery started to rise in the 16th century among both the black and indigenous slaves. Many escaped the plantations and moved to the interior or created small villages and settlements, called *mocambos*.

Because of the overgrowth in the inland jungles, the indigenous tribes, who knew the land well, were able to hide fairly easily. European adventurers called *BANDEIRANTES* went into the interior in search of gold and natives to enslave. They were unsuccessful in capturing many of the tribal people, though. Hence, they relied more upon the African slave trade.

The tribes of Brazil were normally competitive and warlike. However, the abuse of the Portuguese colonists resulted in widespread rebellions by the native peoples. Between 1554 and 1567, the Tupinambá tribe organized and formed a coalition called the Tamoyo Confederation, which was headed by Cunhambebe, a Tupinambá chief.

The French in Brazil came to the assistance of the Tupinambá, and the war between the two factions eventually phased into a war between the Portuguese and the French. In 1567, due to the intervention of two Jesuit missionaries, Manuel de Nóbrega and José de Anchieta, a peace treaty was drawn up between Cunhambebe and the colonists.

To counteract the French intrusion, the Portuguese built forts in the area. Due to the heavy defensive efforts of the Portuguese, the French withdrew but held on to a few isolated ports, which they used to trade.

The Dutch Incursion

Meanwhile, back in Europe, the king of Portugal, Dom Sebastião (Sebastian), disappeared during a war between Portugal and the Moors in North Africa in 1578. The king of Spain, King Philip II, who was also Sebastião's uncle, took advantage of the fact that Sebastião had no heirs. He founded the Iberian Union in 1580 after becoming the king of Portugal himself, although he would not be crowned until the following year. The Iberian Union was the proclaimed union between Spain and Portugal, which placed all of the Iberian Peninsula and Portugal's overseas colonial holdings into the hands of Spain. However, the empires were legally distinct, which allowed Portugal and its colonies to pursue their own interests.

In 1602, Holland and Portugal went to war over the dominion of Brazil. On the Dutch side, it mostly involved their two merchant organizations, the Dutch East India Company and the Dutch West India Company. They raised a military force and chopped away at the expansive Portuguese Empire, as it was then called. Because the war was fought mostly over sugar, it was dubbed the Spice War. This conflict dragged on until 1663, and it was a far-flung affair, including islands and countries outside of South America. While the fighting continued, the Dutch, who were rooted in the area, developed a lucrative sugar trade.

By 1612, Pernambuco produced 14,000 tons of sugar. In 1629, a Dutch fleet under Captain Antonio Vaz gained control of Pernambuco, and Captain Hendrick Corneliszoon Lonck seized its sister city of Olinda. From 1630 onward, the Dutch Republic, financed mostly by the Dutch West India Company, gained control of the northern section of Brazil. In 1637, it was renamed New Holland and was run by an administrative body consisting of both

Dutch and Brazilian administrators. The Brazilian members were Brazilian-born Portuguese, and they represented the colonial population, which had been growing rapidly.

Many new European settlers went to the Portuguese areas to live, as they were given the freedom to worship; the Spanish required their people to adhere by the Catholic faith. Calvinists who were harassed in England came to Brazil, and Catholic missionaries flocked there as well. The population around 1640 consisted of Portuguese, the Brazilian-born Portuguese, those of mixed ethnic origin, African slaves and their children, and the new Dutch immigrants. However, as early as 1642, the Dutch population of Brazil had decreased. Most of the work in Brazil was concentrated on sugar, but it was an abusive economic system dependent upon African slavery, and The Dutch couldn't afford to buy slaves.

In 1645, the planters who were operating under the administration of the Dutch openly rebelled. The revolt mainly took place at the capital of Pernambuco, Recife, and was caused by the moneylenders who had grown increasingly corrupt and were charging unreasonably high-interest rates. The Portuguese took advantage of that to try to regain control over Brazil.

At the Second Battle of Guararapes in 1649, the Dutch military was mostly composed of mercenaries from Germany. The Germans had little interest in defending Brazil, but the native and colonial fighters were passionately fighting for their land. What's more, Dutch soldiers wore heavy armor with brightly-colored clothing and foolishly conducted battle in the torrid Amazon jungle. The native people and colonists knew the jungles well and fought a guerilla-style war. The Brazilians had Henrique Dias and António Filipe Camarão among their generals. Dias was a Brazilian who was the son of one of the original African slaves who'd settled there, and Camarão was from the Potiguara tribe. According to an eyewitness named Michiel van Goch, the Portuguese soldiers were familiar with the terrain and overcame the natural obstacles one might find in a jungle environment. As one might be able to surmise, the Portuguese soundly defeated the Dutch, signifying the end of Dutch occupation.

Back in Europe, hostilities among the countries and vacillating power shifts caused the English to pass the Navigation Acts in 1651. These acts halted all foreign trade through English ports, which deeply affected the Dutch economy. By the year 1654, Holland was no longer a power in South America, and the Portuguese reclaimed their forts in the area.

Because of the conflicts, much of the Brazilian land was devastated, as the armies engaged scorched-earth tactics, ruining many of the plantations. This destroyed both the Portuguese and the Dutch interests in the sugar industry. By 1690, Brazil only supplied 10 percent of the sugar sold in the trade markets. Consequently, it had to endure a recovery period, but sugar still strongly affected the destiny of the Americas.

El Dorado

In South America, the Bandeirantes, or adventure-seekers, had been exploring the northern portion of the continent since the 16th century. They were in search of potential products that could enrich Portugal, Spain, and indeed all of Europe. The Bandeirantes explored the Amazon River and the lands in current-day Brazil, Venezuela, Guyana, and Colombia, and they even traveled high in the Andes. For many years, legends about El Dorado, a legendary city in South America, circulated. It came from the story about tribal chiefs of the Muisca people, as it was said that they would engage in inauguration ceremonies in which each was covered with gold dust. They would then jump into Lake Guatavita to cleanse their bodies, and their subjects would throw in precious jewels as offerings to the god of the deep. The legend grew as time went on, and it eventually transformed into the tale of the empire of El Dorado, which was made of gold.

Early explorers in South America often met indigenous tribesmen with leaders that were adorned with gold jewelry. These native peoples rarely ever revealed their secrets to the location of such gold, which only served to whet the appetites of the gold-hungry Europeans. In fact, in 1545, Spaniards sent an expedition under Hernán Pérez de Quesada to dredge Lake Guatavita in search of it! As it was a very deep mountain lake in the Andes, he was unsuccessful, especially since he only used buckets.

However, in 1580, Antonio de Sepúlveda employed 8,000 people to drain the lake, and they were actually able to lower the lake by six feet. They used a technique in which they created openings on the side of the lake. After many people died due to a collapse of the openings, the foolhardy project was canceled.

That wasn't the end, though. In the late 16th century, Juan Martinez spread the story of a city made of gold called Manoa. Searches were financed, but the legendary city was never found. Many have tried to find El Dorado, including Walter Raleigh, a well-known English explorer, but none have succeeded. Although El Dorado may not be real, it still lives on in the imaginations of today due to the abundance of literary works, movies, video games, and other media made about it.

Venezuela

The Mesoamericans from Central America migrated down to Venezuela from around 5000 BCE to 1000 CE, according to the artifacts that have been carbon dated. The western areas of current-day Venezuela were highlands that were terraced for the growing of maize. To the east lay the llanos, or the flooded grasslands. In the east, the population consisted of hunter-gatherers. The common animals in this area were jaguars, monkeys, bears, anteaters, deer, and armadillos. There were also crocodiles and snakes, including the huge anaconda, a variety of the boa constrictor.

Tribes that formed in this area were the Lokono, the Kalina, and the Timoto-Cuica. The Lokono, also referred to as Arawaks by the early Europeans, were clever with agriculture and mixed their soil with charcoal as a type of fertilizer. They lived in ringed villages.

Oil seeped to the surface in Venezuela, and its use as a fuel was harnessed early on by the natives. The Lokono created primitive heating containers from it. For those who fished, the oil was a godsend as it could be used to caulk their boats and make them waterproof. It was also used medicinally to treat colds, coughs, and burns.

The Kalina people, also known as the Caribs or Mainland Caribs, settled in the Venezuelan region but migrated northeast to settle in today's countries of Guyana, Suriname, French Guiana, and Brazil. They had their own language, which differed from that of the Lokono. They fought with the Lokono in order to gain possession of the areas around the eastern Amazon River and southward to its tributary, the Orinoco River.

The Timoto-Cuica people was a federation named after the two main tribes that composed it—the Timote and the Cuica—although other tribes were a part of the federation. These people were acclimated to living in the heights and foothills of the Andes Mountains. They were an agricultural group of hard-working individuals who grew potatoes and ullucus, a root vegetable. They invented a bread called *arepa*, which is still common in both Venezuelan and Colombian cuisines. The Timoto-Cuica were also master weavers who made clothing and textiles for housing.

Spanish Colonization of Venezuela 1502–1810

Once pearls were discovered along the northeastern coasts, the jamboree started. Spanish ships poured in from Europe and enslaved the indigenous population along the shore to harvest the pearls. By 1521, the supply was nearly exhausted, and the Spanish moved on. The country was named Venezuela by the Spanish explorer Alonso de Ojeda. It means "Little Venice," and it was named this because of the many waterways that penetrated its northeastern coast.

In 1528, Venezuela became a colony of Germany. It was ceded to the Germans to pay off a debt incurred between the Augsburg family and Charles I of Spain. The Germans had heard the rumors of the golden city of El Dorado. They seriously believed that tale, especially after seeing native leaders wearing gold jewelry. In the foolhardy attempt to find El Dorado, their great city of Cumaná, its capital, was left unprotected while Georg von Speyer and Philipp von Hutten searched the interior of the German territory. They were joined by Bartholomeus VI Welser, a member of the illustrious banking family that had an interest in the ownership of the colony. Von Speyer actually became ill during this exploration and had to return to Europe.

While they were away, Spain claimed the right to appoint their own governor, who executed von Hutten and Welser upon their return. During the 16th century, more and more Spaniards moved in and settled there.

Gold!

In 1632, gold was discovered in Yaracuy, which led to the digging of many deep gold mines into the rocks of the Andes. The Spanish overlords enslaved the indigenous peoples who hadn't fled south. Gold mining in those days was such a labor-intensive process that thousands of African slaves were shipped over to help as well.

The overseas trade routes grew between Venezuela and Europe, as Venezuela marketed the gold in exchange for furniture, glassware, and other goods.

The more fortunate natives were subsumed into the feudal society run by the Spanish landowners. They imported horses, which interbred with the native breed, called Criollos. The natives established ranches and made use of the horses to tend to their crops grown on the llanos grasslands. Haciendas sprouted up all over the plains, and each had a hierarchy and structure of its own, modeled after those in Spain.

Venezuela was divided into two viceroyalties, that of Peru and New Spain. Because of the avarice of the investors, more attention was paid to gold and silver mining than to agriculture.

The cocoa bean grew plentifully there and became one of their exports, as well as being used for domestic consumption. Cocoa butter was used to produce solid chocolate and was naturally sweet but with a "bittersweet" taste. When the seeds were ground up, they weren't sweet but needed a sweet additive like vanilla. The sweet pulp of the cocoa bean could be fermented into a very mild alcoholic beverage.

The Royal Guipuzcoan Company of Caracas, a Spanish Basque trading company from north-central Spain, was established in 1728 and controlled the export trade of cocoa, which was highly prized in Europe and provided Venezuela, and the Company, with a source of steady income. Cocoa plantations lay all across the plains, and more African slaves were imported to man the fields. The Venezuelans also grew tobacco, which was a lucrative export as well.

Education and Commerce

Many of the natives who fled from the huge influx of the Spanish colonists migrated south and west. During the 17th century, the Capuchin and the Franciscan friars established missions. There, they taught them Spanish grammar and language courses.

The city of Caracas was built in 1567, its university was established in 1721, which is one of the oldest universities in the Western Hemisphere. Its most illustrious graduate was Andrés Bello, a humanist, legislator, and philosopher who was born in Caracas.

Government

The Kingdom of Venezuela, also known as the Captaincy General of Venezuela, was established in 1777. Before this, it was under the dominion of the Viceroyalty of New Spain and the Viceroyalty of

New Granada. The Kingdom of Venezuela ran like a military state under a governor and loosely operated under the jurisdiction of the Viceroyalty of New Spain. One division, the intendancy, took care of financial matters, and another, the *Audiencia*, took care of judicial affairs.

Venezuela was divided into provinces, which included Caracas, known as the Venezuela Province; Cumaná, also called New Andalusia; Ecuador; Guyana, which eventually included the islands of Trinidad and Tobago; Maracaibo; and Margarita.

Chapter 6 – South America: Argentina, Uruguay, and Paraguay from Pre-Columbian Times through Colonization

Argentina

The earliest migrations to this area came from the north. The migrants traversed between 7300 and 800 BCE across Beringia from eastern Asia. Archeologists know of that prehistoric date because the indigenous people left their "signatures" there in the form of handprints that have been carbon dated to 7300 BCE. The art was spray-painted using a blow-pipe on a rock in the Cave of Hands in Santa Cruz, located in the northeastern area of Argentina.

The Guarani Tribe

The Guarani in South America were called the "theologians of the forest." They populated mostly Argentina but also lived in Uruguay and Paraguay. Ethnically, the Guarani are related to the Tupiniquim, which can be seen by the similarities in their languages.

According to their creation myth, the great father-god *NAMANDU* created himself by rising from the chaos of the primeval mass. He emerged like a tree, with a crown on his head and his fingers reaching toward the sky. Namandu was the prime mover, the creator god, who gave rise to a collective of living beings called *ayuu*. When he spoke, it was with *ne-e*, the speech of human beings. *NAMANDU* is also known as the "master of words," for he communicates with both the divine and human beings.

To help in his wondrous task of building a civilization, *NAMANDU* had the assistance of nature, personified in *KARAI*, the master of fire (as in the sun); *JAKAIRI*, the master of the fog; and *TUPA*, the master of the sea, which also included rain, thunder, and lightning. Each of these minor gods created their own "mother" to act as a companion. Once the principal parts of the world were in place, *NAMANDU* created man and woman and commanded *KARAI* to place a "flame" into each one and ordered *TUPA* to place a fountain of "freshness" into their hearts.

The Guarani were animists and believed that animals and plants had "souls" and that each of these pantheistic gods had its own function, whether it was for good or for evil.

The Legend of Iguazu Falls

The great Iguazu River meets the Parana River. At that juncture is one of the great natural wonders of the world, the Iguazu Falls, which has many divisions and is wider than both the Niagara Falls in North America and the Victoria Falls in Africa. There is a legend that accounts for the formation of these falls, which was held by the Guarani and a neighboring tribe, the Kaingang. The legend addresses the consequences of betrayal. Naipí, a fair maiden, was promised by the chieftain that she would marry the serpent god Mboi. However, Naipí spots the reflection of the very handsome warrior Tarobá, and the two fell in love. Angered at his betrayal, Mboi pushes his snake-like body deep into the land, violently splitting it in his pursuit of the lovers, so much so that the land was cleaved apart, giving rise to the waterfalls.

The Toba People

The lowlands of Argentina, which is called the Pampas, is like a huge prairie of rolling tall grasses. Its temperature is subtropical in the north, while it is cooler but more arid in the southern areas. The bold and muscular pumas wander these plains, as does their prey: the pampas and brocket deer, pampas fox, and rhea. The rhea is related to the emu and ostrich. There are also dozens of species of rodents and birds. Much of the open land has been lost to farming and fires over the years.

In the early 16th century, the Toba, also referred to as the Qom, were described as being of a "fierce countenance." They walked barefoot and went about naked except in the presence of foreigners. They also wore headdresses and belts and tattooed their bodies. They made their living by hunting and fishing and were some of the finest horsemen on the continent.

The Toba in the north-central area and their related smaller tribes lived in the Gran Chaco, which was once a glorious forest and is estimated to be a quarter of a million miles in size. It crosses the borders of northern Argentina, western Paraguay, eastern Bolivia, and segments of southern Brazil.

The Aónikenk

The Aónikenk, or the Tehuelche, lived in Patagonia, the name of the southernmost area of Argentina. Many fanciful stories about these mysterious people have circulated throughout the years. They were called the "Patagones," meaning "big feet," and that began to be embroidered throughout the ages, as it was later rumored that the Aónikenk were giants. An explorer who came with Ferdinand Magellan exclaimed that an Aónikenk man was *"SO TALL THAT THE TALLEST AMONG US ONLY CAME UP TO HIS WAIST."*

These people were hunter-gatherers and didn't practice agriculture. They hunted mostly for guanaco, which is a camelid, and rhea. The native horses of South America were short and stocky. Once the Spanish came in the 16th century, the Spanish stock interbred with them, creating a taller but brawnier horse that became accustomed to long hours on the pampas and plains. They were and are still called Criollos, and they are a special breed associated with Patagonia, as well as the current-day countries of Brazil, Chile, Peru, and Venezuela.

The Aónikenk lived in tents and were nomadic, following the herds of guanacos as they thundered across the plains. Guanaco skin was used to make moccasins and clothing, and their meat was consumed.

It was said that the Aónikenk people had no religion, but they were actually animists who imparted their beliefs in terms of tales passed from father to son. Many of their stories revolved around fanciful tales about the creation of various breeds of animals.

Colonization of Argentina

A large area around the Río de la Plata was incorporated by the Spanish into the Governate of the Río de la Plata in 1549. The Governate of the Río de la Plata was raised in status to the Viceroyalty of the Río de la Plata in 1776. This included not only the Buenos Aires region of Argentina but also Chile, Paraguay, Uruguay, and most of what comprises current-day Bolivia.

Argentina itself didn't have precious metals so that stunted its economic growth until it could be reshaped into a lucrative port. It became vital for the shipment of goods. The colonists and indigenous peoples set up cattle ranches and exported leather to worldwide markets.

Uruguay

Except for the Guarani· people, smaller tribal units in Uruguay were rendered nearly extinct. Their racial roots were somewhat different from that of the other native peoples that settled in South America. These were the descendants of the Charrúa people, who are today trying to reestablish their ethnic identity, indicating that they are different from other more numerous tribes around them. They were fishermen, hunters, and gatherers, who lived a semi-nomadic existence. There were not that many of them. Many intermarriages occurred among the tribes that were present before 1492, which is the date that Christopher Columbus "discovered" America. Among the non-Guarani people were the Charrúa, Chaná, and Arachán.

The Charrúa were the strongest among them and were described as having high cheekbones, a massive bone structure, and well-developed muscular bodies. Ethnologists consider them a superb example of a human being. They had bronze-colored skin and dark hair. It was rumored that the females were just as strong as the men.

While the Charrúa spoke their own language, a dialect of that language was spoken by the Chaná, a neighboring tribe. The Charrúa group of languages is sadly nearly extinct.

The Arachán are extinct, but it is believed that they immigrated to Uruguay from the highlands of the Incas and sections of the Andes Mountains.

The Portuguese and Spanish: Uruguay and Paraguay 1516– 1542

Both Portugal and Spain had discovered that there was gold in South America, so they were determined to find it south of Brazil as well. The first European explorer of Uruguay, Juan Díaz de Solís, whose exact origin is questioned as to whether he was Portuguese or Spanish, was killed by the natives upon his arrival in 1516. So, basically, all he discovered was the antipathy of the local peoples to intrusions. Many historians believe that he was murdered by members of the Charrúa tribe.

Determined to find more of the rumored riches from South America, Sebastian Cabot, an Italian explorer, was employed by England, and later Spain, to explore South America, most notably Argentina and Uruguay.

As mentioned above, the Treaty of Tordesillas had been signed in 1494, dividing South America between Spain and Portugal. Cabot was specifically hired as a cartographer to explore all of South America. Since the definitive borders of the Treaty of Tordesillas hadn't physically been defined, both Spain and Portugal wanted to settle the matter. What's more, they wanted access to the rumored gold that was thought to be in this region. Like most of the Europeans who came to South America, Cabot was aware the Portuguese were gradually occupying Brazil, so he chose to explore the area now known as Argentina in search of gold. He explored the northern regions of Argentina, and after finding no gold there, Cabot then moved south toward current-day Uruguay.

The Colonization of Uruguay

Sebastian Cabot arrived in today's Uruguay in 1526 at a river called the Río de la Plata. He established good relations with the large Guarani tribe there and traded with them. The area surrounding the Río de la Plata's delta conjoins the Parana River, which slices Argentina from north to south. of the Governate of the Río de la Plata was founded a little over two decades later in 1549.

In 1597, Hernando Arias de Saavedra became the governor of the Governate of the Río de la Plata. He was an admirable figure, and it was said that "only in Hernan Darias has virtue triumphed. Although the Spanish fault him as being inclined always toward the criollos [a pure Spaniard] and mestizos [a person of mixed race], he is an honorable gentleman, for in every rule there is an exception."

Cattle were introduced to the Río de la Plata in 1603. The indigenous people then raised cattle in the pampas, and their herds increased substantially to the point that the people were not only eating guanacos but also beef.

Portugal and Spain were in constant competition for the possession of the colonies in South America, and the two powers both had settlements in Uruguay.

Colonization of Paraguay

One of the governmental divisions of the Viceroyalty of Peru, the Real Audiencia of Charcas, awarded some of the lands of Argentina, Uruguay, Chile, and other small portions of the area to a governor that was elected by the Real Audiencia of Charcas. Domingo Martínez de Irala was the governor of the country later known as Paraguay in 1547. The colonial population included mostly males from various parts of Europe, such as Spain, Germany, France, England, Italy, and Portugal. Later on, Paraguay was incorporated into the Viceroyalty of the Río de la Plata.

Since the large Guarani tribe lived in that area, the European males were encouraged to marry Guarani women. Thus, their offspring became mestizos, that is, people of mixed race. They were of a lower social class, so de Irala persuaded Criollos to settle in Paraguay. Those people then became the elite by virtue of race.

In 1542, Charles V of Spain arbitrarily placed Cabeza de Vaca in charge. The people of Paraguay, who had enjoyed the peaceful reign of de Irala, were incensed and rebelled. Before too long, due to the uprisings of the colonists and smaller indigenous tribes in the interior, they defeated de Vaca and sent him home to Spain in chains.

Although the country was inland, de Irala managed to develop a healthy economy. Textiles were made, and the cattle grazed upon the fertile hills. He then opened trade relations with Peru. De Irala died in 1776 and was replaced by Gonzolo de Mendoza and then

Francisco Ortiz de Vergara. He created three new settlements, but they didn't survive for unknown reasons. Political/religious differences occurred among the Spanish governors who followed, and there was a high turnover. It was peaceful until the settlers were allowed to own and run the lands and their farms. They were expected to take care of the material needs of the indigenous people but failed to do so, and many of the Guarani became enslaved. As one might expect, uprisings broke out.

Although Paraguayan Jesuits intervened and created a better system of distribution for food and wealth, it was insufficient. In 1811, the Revolt of the Comuneros took place, pitting the more prosperous Paraguayans against the Jesuits and their followers, which also included many poor farmers.

The Paraguayan officials called for aid from Spain to control the uprisings, but Spain gave little heed to Paraguay except to charge them fees and taxes. Therefore, defensive forces had to be homegrown, and many of the colonists were forced to join militias. They were also recruited to quell uprisings in neighboring provinces as well. These fighters were farmers who were forced to neglect their farmlands, and as a result, the whole area became impoverished.

Chapter 7 – South American Wars of Independence

War of Venezuelan Independence, 1810–1823

In 1809, Vicente Emparán was appointed the captain-general of the Captaincy of Venezuela. However, the municipal council there, along with the elite people of Venezuela, preferred a junta to the traditional captaincy arrangement the Spanish overlords had set up. Europe was shaky at the time, as Joseph Bonaparte (Napoleon's brother) was ruling Spain. Emparán decided to step down in 1810, and the Supreme Junta of Caracas was then established. It declared allegiance to Ferdinand VII of Spain, who was imprisoned.

The Venezuelans in the new junta deposed all the old leaders Bonaparte had sent over. The junta gained the support of seven of the ten provinces in Venezuela, but the other provinces declared loyalty to the French under Bonaparte. In 1810, a civil war broke out between the two factions.

The congress of Caracas worked with the junta, and they found popular support for the total independence of Venezuela. Francisco de Miranda and Simón de Bolívar, who would later play an important role in other independence movements, lent their vigor to help the Venezuelans organize their new government.

The First Republic of Venezuela, 1811–1812

The Venezuela Congress moved ahead, despite opposition, and created the First Republic of Venezuela in 1811. To quell the civil opposition, troops were sent into the wayward provinces that were still loyal to France. Two of those provinces did not succumb, but the province of Valencia did. Spain then sent ships that blockaded the harbors. However, they were interrupted by an earthquake in 1812. At this point, Miranda was appointed dictator in order to keep order.

Two major battles erupted—one in La Victoria and another in San Mateo—and Miranda's troops lost both of them. There was no other choice for him but to sign an armistice. Spanish Captain Domingo de Monteverde became the new captain-general, and he imprisoned many Venezuelans, which went against the cease-fire that had been signed.

Second Republic of Venezuela, 1813–1814

Another Venezuelan patriot, Santiago Mariño, who was incensed by the cruelty of Monteverde, invaded the northeastern territories and began freeing them in 1813. Mariño and his troops eventually based his troops at the city of Cumaná, located about 500 miles east of Caracas. Caracas was the end goal for the revolutionaries, as it was the capital of Venezuela. However, Mariño was not the only revolutionary seeking Venezuelan independence.

In 1813, Bolívar also entered Venezuela with allies. They crossed the Andes and invaded from the west. On August 6th, 1813, Bolívar entered Caracas, declaring the new republic of Venezuela. Of course, Mariño did not agree with this, and he set up his own political entity in eastern Venezuela.

Soon after the new republic was created, a man named José Tomás Boves began a rebellion. He represented the *pardos*, who were people of mixed descent. Boves and his followers objected to the restoration of the republic. The people saw the actions of Bolívar and Mariño as playing into the hands of the elites. Boves, on the other hand, was determined to create his own royalist state and capitalized on these feelings. He invaded from the south and headed toward Caracas.

In order to keep the independence movement alive, Bolívar and Mariño joined forces. However, they were beaten back in 1814 by Boves and had to flee to the east. In the meantime, a Spanish general, Francisco Tomás Morales, arrived to help Boves restore Spanish control, but Boves soon died in the Battle of Urica. Despite his death, the royalists won, and Morales assumed control of the Captaincy of Venezuela.

Bolívar's Attempts

In 1815, Bolívar fled to numerous areas in search of help. By 1816, he was ready to try again. He was fairly successful in this endeavor, but Pablo Morillo, the leader of the Spanish forces at the time, was also successful. Thus, the two sides entered into a stalemate.

Despite this, in 1819, Bolívar declared a new republic, the Republic of Great Colombia, whose territory included not only Venezuela but also New Granada. More people began to support Bolívar and his efforts, and slowly, the tide began to turn against the Spanish.

New Granada

Bolívar moved into the region of New Granada in 1819, hot off the victories he had enjoyed against the Spanish. The Battle of Boyacá was another resounding victory for Bolívar and his forces, and with that victory came the end of the Spanish occupation in New Granada.

The liberation of New Granada gave Bolívar an excellent base from which to attack Venezuela, and soon afterward, he launched a fresh attack against Morillo's forces.

Bolívar envisioned New Granada and Venezuela as one large territory, and in 1819, he made that dream come true by declaring the Republic of Colombia (Gran Colombia), which united both New Granada and Venezuela. This unification was more of a way to fight against the Spanish as a unified front, though. Over time, Gran Colombia would come to include several South American countries who were searching for their own independence. In 1831, Gran Colombia was no more, and the territories that were left (which consist of modern-day Colombia, Ecuador, and Venezuela) split apart. In 1903, Colombia would split apart again, creating the modern-day state of Panama.

However, it should be noted that the war for Venezuela's independence ended in 1823. The Spanish tried one last time to regain the territory after the creation of Gran Colombia, but they failed. After this, Gran Colombia assisted other South American countries in their fight for independence.

Independence of Argentina, 1810–1818

In 1808, the king of Spain abdicated the throne during the Peninsular War, handing it over to Napoleon Bonaparte, who allowed his brother to rule. The Spanish wouldn't go down without a fight and opposed this move, creating juntas (Spanish for council or committee). However, the French were too strong to contend with, and the northern half of the country fell into French hands. The Supreme Junta, which had been formed by the smaller juntas that popped up throughout Spain, was dissolved in January 1810.

News of this reached Buenos Aires in May, where Balthasar Hidalgo de Cisneros was the Spanish-appointed Viceroy of the Río de la Plata, which, as you might remember, oversaw the modern-day territories of Argentina, Chile, Bolivia, Paraguay, and Uruguay. Soon after, a revolt ensued, called the May Revolution, which affected not only Argentina but also Paraguay and Uruguay. A group of lawyers and military commanders had created their own junta, in which they decided not to recognize the new ruling body in Spain. With that move, the Viceroyalty of the Río de la Plata fell apart, and Hidalgo Cisneros was forced to resign. A new governmental body was set up under the auspices of Spain, which was called the Primera Junta.

The Primera Junta divided into factions between Cornelio Saavedra and Mariano Moreno. Saavedra prevailed and appointed more members to the junta, outnumbering the supporters of Moreno.

The Primera Junta was renamed the Junta Grande and created local juntas in other cities. News of this reached the notable general José de San Martín, who had been fighting in Europe and rushed over to help Argentina fight for the cause of independence in 1812. He met up with Commander Manuel Belgrano, a Creole of mixed blood, who led the patriot forces against the royalist forces in the Andes. Belgrano scored many victories but was eventually defeated. San Martín then stepped in and took his place.

Since the May Revolution impacted so many countries, the end of the Argentine War for Independence coincided with Chile's fight for independence. In 1814, San Martín realized he could attack the Viceroyalty of Peru by attacking the ruling body of Chile, the Captaincy of Chile. In 1818, San Martín was successful in driving back the Spanish with the Battle of Maipú. Although this battle was not the end of the Chilean War of Independence, it was the end of Argentina's efforts in the war, as Peruvian forces began aiding the Chileans instead. Argentina also played a role in the independence of Paraguay, as Argentina insisted that Paraguay become their dependent province. Although Paraguay supported Argentinian independence, they resented having Argentina rule them. Commander Manuel Belgrano attempted to enforce this upon Paraguay in 1810, but he severely underestimated the patriotic spirit of the Paraguayans. In 1811, Paraguay declared its fight for independence.

Independence of Paraguay, 1811

The independence of Paraguay also began with the May Revolution. Shortly after the revolution, Governor José de Espinola y Peña attempted to bring Paraguay into the fold of the Primera Junta. Peña had ties with the former governor, Lázaro de Rivera, who had executed hundreds of citizens, mostly Paraguayans. As a result, Paraguay rebelled against the Argentinian army. The later expeditions of Manuel Belgrano didn't fare much better.

In July 1810, two Paraguayan military captains, Pedro Juan Cabellero and Fulgencio Yegros, rose up. They created a plan for what is known as the Revolution of May 14, in which they deposed the Spanish governor and declared the independence of Paraguay in 1811. The Paraguayan Republic was established two years later in 1813; however, Paraguay did not officially declare its independence until 1842. Even then, other countries didn't accept it, with some, such as Argentina and the United States, taking as long as a decade to officially recognize its independence.

Independence of Uruguay, 1811–1828

The fight for independence in Uruguay also began with the ideas that sprouted from the May Revolution of 1810, as well as the dissolution of the Viceroyalty of the Río de la Plata. In February 1811, José Gervasio Artigas and his followers declared an open war against the Spanish. With the help of the military from Buenos Aires, Artigas was successful in repelling the Spanish—that is, until the Spanish asked the Portuguese from Brazil to assist them in their efforts against the rebels, which caused Buenos Aires to withdraw their help. Artigas and his supporters retreated, leaving Uruguay in the hands of the royalists, but in 1813, Artigas returned again, aiding José Rondeau during the Second Siege of Montevideo. After this victory, Artigas helped form the League of Free Peoples, which was the union of those provinces that wanted to be free from Spanish rule.

This League scared the Portuguese in Brazil, as Uruguay was situated right next to it. So, in 1816, the Brazilian forces invaded, hoping to destroy Artigas and his followers. By late January 1817, the Brazilian army held Montevideo. It most likely seemed as if that would be the end of Uruguay's plans for freedom, especially when Artigas's forces were defeated once and for all in 1820. However, the end of the Brazilian War for Independence in 1824 helped propel Uruguay further along its own path for independence.

In 1824, the city of Montevideo was freed from Portuguese control due to the efforts of the Brazilians seeking freedom from Europe. Juan Antonio Lavalleja, a revolutionary leader and politician, campaigned for the independence of Uruguay as being separate from Brazil in April 1825. For 500 days, they waged war over the issue. Neither side appeared to be winning, so the parties agreed to discuss the matter. In 1828, the Treaty of Montevideo was drawn up, which established the official state of Uruguay. Like Paraguay, though, Uruguay's independence wasn't accepted right away.

Independence of Chile, 1810–1826

The governor of Chile, Garcia Carrasco, antagonized the people as soon as he took over in 1808. After Carrasco was implicated in a political scandal, the populace pressured for him to be ousted. The people themselves then set up the First Junta in 1810 and required that the people take a loyalty oath to the king. Three political groups sprung from that: the extremists, the moderates, and the royalists. Of the three, only the extremists wanted a path to total independence, albeit a gradual one. The extremists and the moderates wanted some form of local elections, while the royalists were content with the status quo.

Voting was held in the major cities of Chile except for Santiago. As the election moved along, it became clear that Santiago would cast the deciding vote. Then Tomás de Figueroa, a strident royalist, triggered a revolt in Santiago. The revolt failed, and he was executed shortly afterward. When the latecomer José Miguel Carrera arrived from Spain, he conspired with others to dismantle support for the moderates, which was the most popular faction at the time, and launched two coups, which were both crushed. However, at the end of 1811, Carrera took over as a dictator, albeit with some liberal tendencies.

In the meantime, the National Assembly was in place, and its elected members came from the various factions of the political spectrum. Combined with the pro-independence media, the unrest continued. Carrera eventually resigned due to political pressure and general incompetence and fled the country.

In 1813, the viceroy of Peru, José Fernando de Abascal, who had jurisdiction over Chile, sent in a fleet under the command of Mariano Osorio to restore order. The Treaty of Lircay was signed in May of 1814 but was essentially ignored, even by the administration. The commander of the forces, Mariano Osorio, pushed farther south and squashed the rebellion in Santiago, restoring royal control.

By 1817, two patriot leaders, Bernardo O'Higgins and the aforementioned José de San Martín, formed an army, made the treacherous climb over the Andes, swarmed into the area around Santiago, and defeated the royalists under Osorio and Rafael Maroto. O'Higgins was appointed the supreme director of Chile. Although he was the longest-lasting supreme director, he was forced to abdicate his position in 1823, after which he left Chile.

In 1818, the royalist commander Osorio was then sent to the city of Conception, near Santiago, but was confronted with the forces of the patriot San Martín, who proved to be victorious.

There were only two royalist strongholds still left: some fortifications at the city of Valdivia in southern Chile and the island of Chiloe. In 1824, the Battle of **Ayacucho** resulted in the expulsion of the royalists from Valdivia. Chiloe was more difficult for the rebels to conquer, but they made several attempts. Two attempts were unsuccessful, but the royalist forces left in 1826. Although the independence of Chile wasn't recognized until 1844, it was instilled in Chiloe with the departure of the royal troops.

Independence of Peru, 1811–1824

Around 1808, junta movements began to erupt. These movements were triggered by political and economic events. The lower classes staged uprisings because of racial discrimination and governmental corruption. When the mining industry declined, the people of the area split ideologically between Upper Peru and the southern region.

In 1811, Francisco Antonio de Zela, a Peruvian-born leader of mixed blood, led an armed rebellion against the Spanish overlords in the southern city of Tacna. This rebellion paralleled the revolt going on in neighboring Argentina at the time, so the Argentinians agreed to send de Zela extra forces. Unfortunately, though, those troops never reached de Zela because the Argentinian rebels were defeated at the Battle of Huaqui. Because of that, and the capture of de Zela, this initial Peruvian rebellion failed.

In 1812, the natives in Huánuco also wanted to free themselves from the clutches of Spain. The rebellion was under the leadership of Juan Jose Castelli, a native-born Argentinian, but it failed. However, these movements did bring about unity between the two regions. Class divisions faded, as the majority of both the wealthy and poorer classes had the same goal—to free themselves from Spanish rule.

From 1814 to 1815, another rebellion broke out, this time led by the city administrators in Cusco and the Criollos – that is, the wealthier societal segment –and the remarkable leader Mateo Pumacahua, who wanted the reforms recommended by the Spanish Constitution of 1812. Their battles were met with some mixed results, but Pumacahua united with the Criollo leaders when Spain made no moves to reform. He then formed a junta. It was, however, crushed by the royalist forces in 1815, and Pumacahua was executed.

In 1820, Spanish-Argentinian General José de San Martín, who sought independence for all of South America, brought his battle northward from Chile. They staged an amphibious landing by the Peruvian Liberation Expedition, and he and his rebels captured the province of Ica. San Martín attempted to negotiate with the viceroy, Joaquín de la Pezuela, but talks broke down.

Hostilities ensued, and General Juan Antonio Álvarez de Arenales moved into Upper Peru and defeated the royalists at the Battle of Cerro de Pasco. From there, the patriots attacked two port cities: Arica and Tacna. The patriot forces inland drove the royalists into the highlands before pulling back. In late June 1821, San Martín entered Lima and offered the residents their independence. They were anxious to be independent of Spain, and the Act of Independence was soon signed the summer of 1821.

Creation of Bolivia, 1825

In 1810, there were royalist strongholds within Upper Peru, a sector of Peru that extended east and southeast of today's Peru. However, the majority of people in this region were under rebel control. The royalists were led by Pedro Antonio Olañeta, and the rebels followed the lead of the patriot, Simón Bolívar and Antonio José de Sucre. Olañeta had the support of the Criollos, the elite class who carried Spanish blood. In 1824, the royalists were defeated at the Battles of Junín and Ayacucho. Olañeta refused to release his power, so, in 1825, he was killed fighting his own men, who had defected to the other side. With this move, Spanish rule was eliminated in Upper Peru. What's more, Spain had effectively lost its control of Peru and the rest of continental South America.

Upper Peru became Bolivia, named after Simón Bolívar, who is viewed as a national hero along with José de San Martín, among others. Through a series of radical reforms, Bolívar made all of his citizens free and equal, established land reforms, and distributed land to the natives, from whom it had been confiscated by Spain in the first place. He also eliminated the tribute taxes that were paid to Spain and established a fair tax system.

However, due to the rebellions and the war of independence, Bolivia was in a severe financial crisis. Bolívar handed over the administration to his former partner, Antonio José de Sucre. Sucre struggled to remedy the economic decline, but recovery was slow coming. After an assassination attempt, Sucre resigned.

In 1829, Sucre was succeeded by Andrés de Santa Cruz y Calahumana. Santa Cruz made financial readjustments that greatly alleviated the economic crisis, and Bolivia moved into a promising future.

Independence of Brazil, 1822

The *Cortes* was a liberal constituent assembly of elected officials that ruled Brazil, whose members vigorously supported a constitutional monarchy. In 1821, the *Cortes* supported King Dom John VI of Portugal. He placed his son, Dom Pedro, as a regent to rule the colony of Brazil in March 1821. Pedro guaranteed many rights for the people and reduced taxes. The Portuguese lieutenant general, Jorge Avilez, had other plans for Brazil, and he tried to instigate a mutiny in June. Avilez insisted that Pedro sign an agreement that said Pedro would always honor the Portuguese Constitution. In the end, Pedro, more or less, essentially granted Avilez the real power to rule. The *Cortes* issued a decree that placed Brazil under the authority of the Portuguese king in September of the same year, which basically made Dom Pedro the governor of the province, but the Brazilians had become accustomed to more autonomy, and so, they objected. Fortunately, however, Prince Dom Pedro himself was still a liberal and didn't oppose their views. He earned the label "the Liberator," as the people looked to him to free them from Portuguese dominion. The *Cortes* also denounced José Bonifacio, who was essentially Pedro's right-hand man. So, when the *Cortes* dissolved its colonial government in Rio de Janeiro in

September, Prince Pedro, who was determined to hold his ground this time, made a dramatic move.

Pedro, along with Bonifacio and their many followers, fought back against Avilez, who eventually was forced to surrender. Dom Pedro tried to maintain ties with Portugal, but the cracks that had formed between the nation and its colonies were too many and too big to fix. On September 7th, 1822, after hearing that the *Cortes* stripped him of his rights to rule, Prince Dom Pedro mounted his horse and, in full uniform, rode in front of his Guard of Honor. Pedro boldly pronounced, *"FRIENDS, THE PORTUGUESE CORTES WISHED TO ENSLAVE AND PERSECUTE US. AS OF TODAY, OUR BONDS ARE ENDED. BY MY BLOOD, BY MY HONOR, BY MY GOD, I SWEAR TO BRING ABOUT THE INDEPENDENCE OF BRAZIL. BRAZILIANS, LET OUR WATCHWORD FROM THIS DAY FORTH BE 'INDEPENDENCE OR DEATH!'"*

Pedro received remarkable support from the Brazilians. Brazil marks its Independence Day on September 7th, but Prince Pedro became the emperor later in the year, on October 12th. His official title was Dom Pedro I, the Constitutional Emperor and Perpetual Defender of Brazil. This action was met with much hostility from the members of the *Cortes*, who favored Portuguese dominance.

The War of Brazilian Independence, 1822-1824

One may think the problem was over, that Brazil was finally independent, but that was not the case. Pedro's dominion only extended over a few provinces, and he realized war would have to be waged to place all of Brazil under his control.

In January 1822, skirmishes broke out between Portuguese soldiers and the local militias in the port cities of Salvador—the capital of the state of Bahai—São Luis, Belém, and Montevideo, the capital of today's Uruguay. The Portuguese troops stopped the progress of the local Brazilian militias in those cities, but most of the other rural cities were loyal to Brazil.

The Brazilians desperately needed naval warships, as most of what they had in stock were in an extreme state of disrepair. Because Britain was wary about taking sides in the upcoming battles, Dom Pedro personally had to sign for 350 new ships to be constructed for Brazil by British shipbuilders.

Pedro then hired British Admiral Thomas Cochrane to head up his forces. Cochrane had much experience in military affairs, as he had fought in the Napoleonic Wars. Initially, Cochrane had difficulty due to sabotage by sailors who were loyal to Portugal, which delayed their entry into the battle zone. Fortunately, Dom Pedro was able to have his ships built and his navy purged of malcontents and seamen that supported Portugal. Instead of those men, Brazil used slaves, freemen, and native Brazilians, as well as mercenaries, to man their ships.

The Battle of Jenipapo

In the northern province of Piauí, Major João José de Cunha Fidié led the Portuguese troops against the Brazilians under Leonardo Branco. As the Brazilians had been tasked with ridding their forces of Portuguese-allied soldiers, they had to rely upon untrained and inexperienced fighters. Those fighters used primitive weapons, including spears, axes, and even sickles, to ward off the Portuguese, who wielded superior weapons and boasted trained forces. The Brazilians were unsuccessful, and as a result, Brazil lost control of its northern perimeter on March 13th, 1823.

Siege of Caxias

The Siege of Caxias was fought from late May to late July 1823, and it marked the turning point of the war. Over the months, Brazil made vigorous attempts to arm and update their armed forces, recruiting only the most experienced men for their campaigns. During the Siege of Caxias, which was located in Maranhão, the Brazilians fought hard to reduce the number of Portuguese troops defending Caxias. By July of 1823, the Portuguese, whose numbers had been significantly reduced, surrendered.

Siege of Salvador

To gain control of the crucial city of Salvador, Dom Pedro utilized a hand-selected, elite unit called the Emperor's Battalion. José Joaquim de Lima e Silva was the commanding officer. Salvador, the capital of the Bahia province, was infested with people who had mixed loyalties. The Brazilians had the aid of a French Brigadier officer named Pierre Labatut and a promising cadet by the name of Luís Alves de Lima e Silva, the grandson of the aforementioned José Joaquim. The Siege of Salvador lasted over a year, beginning in March 1822 and ending in July 1823. During that time, many of Labatut's officers betrayed the Brazilians. They were removed from the fighting, imprisoned, and then sent to Rio de Janeiro. De Silva's loyalty was also questioned, but the issue remained unresolved, and so, he remained in the fight.

Luís Alves conducted three very forceful raids upon the Portuguese, who tried to maintain a stranglehold on the city. All of his efforts were successful, and by the end of the siege, the Portuguese had lost a staggering number of men. In the end, the Brazilians were successful, and they entered the city in victory.

Chapter 8 –The Natives in North America (13,000 BCE–1492 CE)

Native North Americans

The ancients trudged along the cold land bridge Beringia and entered a new land—the continent of North America. It was a new land, a new earth. It was born of what the Iroquois called the "Sky World." In the middle of the Sky World, a great tree grew. The wife of the great ruler Ha-wen-ni-yu asked for a sample of the root of this great tree. He reluctantly dug a hole to tear a piece of the root for her. However, the root left a hole, which grew wider and wider. It led down to the bowels of the earth, and the Sky Woman, Ata-en-sic, fell in.

Downward and downward, she plunged. With great concern, the creatures of the waters below looked upon her and called to the wind and other water creatures to help. Large-winged birds formed a feathery raft to support her. Then the muskrat looked for a creature that could live on both the land and the water.

A giant turtle came by, and it was upon his great back that a new land was built. The turtle bore the sacred name of Hah-nu-nah. Ata-en-sic placed mud upon the turtle's back, and it grew. Then she stepped onto the land she created and sprinkled dust into the air, creating the stars.

Pre-Columbian Era (13,000 BCE–1492 CE)

Prehistorical migrations came from the west, and some of the people crossed the continent and made their homes in the east and south. Groups of people from northern Asia and Siberia crossed the ice bridge of Beringia and moved eastward, populating most of what is now Canada and the United States. Later on, the Norsemen came from the east into Iceland and Greenland.

Branches of these huge migrations, which took place over centuries, followed the western coast of North America and settled in Mesoamerica (Central America), with some then moving down to South America.

The Paleoindians

The people carrying these creation stories migrated from the ice-laden land bridge and moved gradually southeast when the great glaciers melted. Some of the people stayed there and built settlements.

Many large animals populated these areas and waters like the great hairy mammoths, the American mastodon, bison, the great walruses, whales, and seals.

Radiocarbon dating indicates that the earliest human ancestor of the Americas created the first human settlement in today's central Montana. Artifacts like stone-shaped projectiles and arrowheads were found sprinkled all over that region. The Paleoindians used "lithic" tools, which were created from stone. Arrows and axes were made by laboriously flaking away at stones to shape the weapon into a point. Then they were fastened on to a sapling and tied with stiff vines or smaller branches. The men hunted in pairs or in groups, as the animals they hunted were very large.

The Kennewick Man

In 1996, the skeleton of a Paleoindian man was found in the state of Washington, located in the northwest of the United States. After many forensic and clinical investigations, it was determined by most that the individual was related to the Polynesian people of Southeast Asia and/or perhaps even the Ainu people, who were the indigenous people of Japan. According to anthropologists, the Kennewick Man was not an ancestor of the Native Americans nor the ancient Europeans, such as the Norsemen, who came over the Atlantic to Greenland.

The Kennewick Man was nearly six feet tall and heavily muscular. The bones were slightly bowed, which seems to be evidence of heavy activity. He appears to have thrived on the consummation of fish and marine mammals, and there is biochemical evidence that he may have even migrated to Alaska during his hunts.

There is also evidence that he had been hit by an arrow, possibly meaning there was a conflict among tribal clans. Even though he was only 38 years old at the time of his death, arthritis was evident, but it wasn't severe.

The Younger Dryas

Geological records show that there was a sudden, unexplained drop in temperature about 10,000 years ago. The warming of the earth halted temporarily, and many of the mammals died, causing a concomitant loss of life among the tribes who hunted them.

Vegetation in the Northeast, which was originally spruce, changed into a mixture of broad-leafed deciduous hardwood trees. As time went on, regions in the southeastern areas became wetter and warmer due to the trapped trade winds blowing up from the equator. When the Younger Dryas period began to subside, the jet stream (westward global winds) moved northward, causing the ice in the lower northern regions to melt and the vegetation to return.

The Native North American Tribes

There were a countless number of tribes that arrived in North America. Tribal groups were identified by the similarities in their languages and other cultural traits, as well as where they settled, and they are generally categorized as:

Paleo-Eskimo/pre-Inuit – includes the Independence I and II cultures, Saqqaq culture of Greenland, and the early Dorsets.

Arctic – includes the Aleutians in current-day Alaska and northern Canada.

Subarctic – includes the Athabaskan tribes in the northwestern area and across current-day Canada.

Northeastern – includes the Iroquois confederacy, the Mohegans, the Hurons, and the Penobscots, who settled in current-day Maine and the Great Lakes region. They also include the Delaware tribal family and the Algonquian-speaking tribes, who settled along the northeastern and eastern coasts and in the surrounding woodlands.

Southeastern – includes the Cherokees, Choctaws, Chickasaws, and Creek confederacy.

The Great Basin and the Great Plains – includes the Sioux, Pawnee, and the Plains Cree.

The Southwestern – includes the Hopi and related agrarian-centered tribes, as well as the Navajo and Apache.

The Far Western – includes the Chinooks. California and the states along the Pacific were a melting pot of over one hundred tribes.

Paleo-Eskimo/pre-Inuit Tribes

These tribes made the migratory route across the ice bridge from Asia to North America prior to the year 3000 BCE. They had their origin in Siberia, so these hardy people were accustomed to the harsh rigors of ice and snow. They moved eastward across the northern part of current-day Canada. Some made settlements along the eastern shore, but others ventured into today's island of Greenland. It's unknown as to whether the Baffin Bay and the Labrador Sea that lie between Canada and Greenland was a solid ice sheet or if these travelers fashioned vessels to cross over to Greenland.

Two cultures established themselves there: the Saqqaq culture of northern Greenland, which was there from the very beginning, around 2500 BCE to 800 BCE, and the Independence cultures, which co-existed with the Saqqaq people from about 2400 BCE to 80 BCE.

For unknown reasons, the Saqqaq culture vanished and was replaced by the Dorset culture. Those people were closely related to the Inuits and Eskimos of the Arctic tribes (see below for more information). They grew and expanded to western Greenland and thrived there between 500 BCE to 1500 CE. The Inuits came to join these sparse settlements around 1200 CE. The Dorset and Inuit civilizations were more advanced culturally. They fashioned lamps, carvings, and specific tools for hunting and butchering seals and sea mammals from soapstone. They also used slate, agate, and quartz to create tools as well.

Arctic Tribes

The Inuits are famous for their igloos, a rounded home built of ice blocks with a hole in the top to let out the smoke from their fires. They kept one doorway, which was covered with animal skins. In the warmer season, they erected houses made of animal bones covered with skins.

They lived mostly on uncooked meat, as they found cooked meat tasteless. Blubber, or fat from sea mammals, was eaten, and they also collected various tubers and grasses, depending on the season and area they lived in. The animals they hunted included polar bears, narwhals (small whales), seals, caribou, and birds. In the warmer months, they grew beans.

They wrapped themselves in parkas made from the fur of the skinned animals. Their main mode of transportation was via dog sled and kayaks made of bark.

There is evidence that these people settled in the Arctic and even the circumpolar regions around 4,000 years ago.

Sub-Arctic Tribes: The Athabaskans

The Athabaskan peoples emerged about 1,300 years ago. They were predominantly nomadic and literally carried their homes with them in the form of animal skins and dried branches. These large family groups traveled throughout Alaska and the related subarctic areas, following herds of caribou and moose. They also designed wooden traps for smaller animals like muskrats, beavers, and Arctic hares.

They built central areas of long wooden houses but wandered far from them, only returning from time to time for feasts or celebrations. Hunters broke up into smaller groups, and food was shared among the people.

The Athabaskans were fur trappers who traded the skins of animals, which others would use as clothing. They traversed the areas north and slightly south of the Great Lakes, eating animal meat and trading with neighboring tribes for beans and clay pottery.

The language of the Athabaskans, which is a part of the larger language group Na-Dene, is related to the languages spoken in Siberia, lending some credence to the belief that some of these people originated from there.

Northeastern Tribes

The peoples who settled in the Northeast learned the language of nature and gained much knowledge from the soil and the woods. They were masters of stalking herds of caribou and varieties of deer. Many could even smell the animals, which is a long-lost art that served them well.

The Iroquois confederacy contained the tribes of the Seneca, Cayuga, Onondaga, Oneida, and Mohawk. They first settled around Lake Ontario but expanded their territory to include the modern-day states of Michigan, Ohio, Pennsylvania, and New York. They also learned the art of raising the "three sisters," which is corn, squash, and beans. As early as 3000 BCE, researchers found remnants of squash. Men raised the crops, while the women prepared the food and raised the children.

The Algonquians were hunter-gatherers who migrated from the northern Canadian regions about 2,000 years ago. They fished the Great Lakes and the multitude of streams and rivers flowing from them. Salmon was plentiful, which they caught with spears. Later on, the Algonquians fashioned nets made of soft saplings and tall grasses. The earth there had a high clay content, which was used to fashion pottery, baskets, and storage containers to save food for use in the winter. They eventually gravitated eastward in what is today the provinces of Quebec and Ontario.

The Native Americans had extensive trade networks. Those in the east would carry their agricultural products and furs westward to trade with the tribes in the Great Plains. The tribes in the plains would compensate by trading copper, silver, large shells, and pearls. The copper and silver could be used for bowls, utensils, and jewelry.

The Iroquois and related tribes gathered in longhouses constructed of tree limbs and straw lined with mud for insulation. They also built wigwams, which were rounded structures, using the same type of materials for single families. In the colder weather, they usually lived in the longhouses for warmth.

There were frequent conflicts between the various tribes over trade. They also engaged in war during droughts. When a tribe lost many of their warriors, they fought "mourning wars," which was intended to replace the warriors they had lost. The men they captured became captives and were like slaves unless they gained rank through their honorable behavior. They would sometimes replace lost family members through kidnapping.

Each tribe enjoyed a degree of autonomy but maintained unity through a federalist system, which balanced the needs of the smaller groups with the needs of the whole nation. The Iroquois confederacy is one of the first known examples of Native Americans unifying in this manner.

Southeastern Tribes

The Southeastern indigenous peoples settled the lands along the Mississippi River between 1000 to 1300 CE. Like the Northeastern tribes, the Southeastern tribes grew beans, squash, and corn. Because the climate was warmer in the Mississippi Valley, they were also able to grow fruit, seeds, tobacco, and nuts. Hunting and fishing in the greater Mississippi region and the Gulf of Mexico supplied their needs for protein.

An urban center known as Cahokia became one of the largest trade capitals of the east. They built primitive "cities" with thatched roofs and were highly organized. Trade routes went up and down the Mississippi and Ohio Rivers and involved the exchange of flint, which was useful for arrowheads, and soapstone, a soft stone easily shaped into containers, bowls, and pots, as well as dugout canoes, furs, and skins.

Society was more hierarchical, and its chiefdoms were based upon heredity. Some tribes, like the Creeks, enslaved people from other tribes and forced them to work the farms for them.

The Great Basin and Plains Tribes

The area of these tribes spread to the east of the Rocky Mountains and eastward toward the Appalachians. It was mostly flatland, full of grasses, sagebrush, and some arid desert areas. This region, settled around the year 1100 CE, was sparsely populated, as it wasn't very fertile. The hunters did manage to eke out a living from the animals and rodents they could shoot and trap.

The American bison traveled in huge herds by the thousands across the Great Plains and migrated with the seasons. They followed watersheds but didn't traverse the lowlands due to the mud and soft soil. Some thrived in the highlands of today's Utah at elevations of 8,000 feet, while others traveled well-worn paths through Ohio.

Legend of the White Buffalo

The indigenous peoples of North America passed along their morals via tales related to nature. Among the Sioux, the legend of the White Buffalo emerged during a time when the people were starving from a lack of buffalo. It is a tale of hope, respect, and rebirth.

In the summer, it was said that two men went out to hunt. They met a beautiful woman dressed in white, who floated when she walked. One man was lecherous and tried to grab her. He was suddenly engulfed by a dark cloud and turned into a pile of bones. The woman looked upon the other man and said, "Return to your people, and tell them I am coming." Then she unwrapped a bundle she carried and gave him a pipe to smoke. She taught him how to use it and told him about the value of the buffalo and the respect they should have for their fellow tribe, the Lakota, with whom they often fought. "You are from Mother Earth," she said. "What you are doing is as great as the warriors do. Smoke it in peace." Then she rolled around four times and turned into a white buffalo calf. After some time passed, the people honored the pipe and ceased fighting, and new laws were passed among the tribes. Shortly thereafter, the buffalo returned, and they were plentiful. This legend had spread from tribe to tribe throughout North America, and each tribe tends to claim it as their own.

The Southwestern Tribes

The indigenous peoples arrived in the Southwest in about 1500 BCE. Originally called the "Anasazi," these tribes were the ancestors of the Pueblo Indians. Their lands extended as far north as the Pacific Northwest down to current-day New Mexico, but they didn't extend westward to the coast.

The Anasazi were cliff-dwellers, and their villages were carved into the cliffs of the sandstone canyons in current-day Utah, western New Mexico, and northern Arizona. The purpose of building their settlements so high up was to protect themselves from the elements, such as the winds, the heat, and the sandstorms. There were numerous mesas upon which they built their villages. Some of the larger settlements built by the Pueblos, who succeeded them, were like high-rise apartment houses with as many as 800 rooms.

There were also settlements on the lower elevations below, and the Pueblos built a series of roads in order to conduct trade with the people who lived along the Rio Grande River.

Because the land was hot and dry, these people developed a sophisticated irrigation system. For that reason, they were able to grow corn and beans. They built elaborate cities and towns with housing built of adobe.

Chaco Canyon, located in northwestern New Mexico, was a center of trade for the tribes. Ruins from that enormous region have been excavated, such as ceremonial stone platforms and raised round marketplaces made of sandstone. Multi-family dwellings have also been found, along with single-family homes in villages. The larger residences sometimes had as many as a hundred rooms. They aligned their buildings and towns with the cardinal directions and had structures indicating the solstices and equinoxes in order to predict the growing and harvesting seasons.

The Navajo, another Southwestern tribe, raised sheep and used the wool for yarn. They developed spinning and weaving, creating elaborate clothing of various colors that were made from plants and minerals. Wars were common, particularly among the Navajo, Comanche, Apache, and Hopi. Warriors from tribal settlements would raid each other to rob and steal goods and food.

The Far Western Tribes

In 8000 BCE, the Pacific Northwest, specifically along the Columbian River, was an ideal place for salmon fishing, whaling, and hunting for seals, sea otters, and shellfish. The smaller villages were composed of wickiups, similar to wigwams, and were made of leaves, brush, and wood. The wickiups were designed to be mobile, while larger buildings were built elsewhere to house and service the markets for trade. In fact, there were many regions of the Far West that built trading centers where the people could exchange goods they couldn't get in their tribal areas. Acorns were used early on as currency.

Agriculture also flourished in this area, as fruits and vegetables had long growing seasons, which the area could accommodate. Some of the indigenous tribes, specifically the Chinooks, engaged in slavery, as they had a lot of crops to plant and harvest.

Chapter 9 – Iceland and Greenland

Iceland, the Irish, and Norse Settlements

In the 7th century CE, it is believed that the first Europeans began to settle in North America. They first came to Iceland, which is why, even though Iceland isn't technically a part of North America, it is briefly included in this section. Soon after settlements appeared in Iceland, Europeans began to voyage to Greenland as well. The people who traversed to these lands were predominantly Norse, although there were Scottish-Irish present. In the old Icelandic sagas, it is said that Scottish-Irish monks inhabited Iceland first.

The monks who first arrived may have been hermits. *The Icelandic Book of Settlements* indicates that the monks left Iceland when the Norsemen arrived in around 870 CE. The text relates that the monks also left behind bells, books, and crosiers, which are the staffs carried by the Christian bishops. No such artifacts were ever found, though.

Iceland was established as a permanent settlement when a Norwegian explorer named Ingólfr Arnarson traveled to the island to build a permanent settlement around 874. However, according to *The Icelandic Book of Settlements*, Arnarson was not the first to discover Iceland. According to the book, the credit goes to a seafarer named Naddod, who supposedly discovered the island around 860. He called it "Snowland." However, the entire island turned green with life once summer hit, causing the name "Snowland," or its later name "Iceland," to be somewhat of a misnomer.

Hrafna-Floki Vilgeroarson, the next explorer who sailed to Iceland, returned to Norway with specimens and information regarding the island. Despite the frigid temperatures of Iceland's winter, which Vilgeroarson described in great detail, more curious settlers migrated there. Ingólfr Arnarson and his wife, Hallveig Fróðadóttir, sailed soon after to create the aforementioned permanent settlement. It was called Reykjavík, which is the capital of Iceland today.

The earliest administrative structure was the Icelandic Commonwealth, which was formed around 930. It was heavily judicial in nature and put decision-making powers in the hands of the chieftains. The Icelandic Commonwealth was created as a response to the autocratic nature of the king of Norway, Harald Fairhair, but it did contain many elements of Norwegian traditions.

Iceland also had a legislative assembly, similar to a parliament. It was called the Alþingi or Althing. Although the chieftains ultimately made the decisions, all free men could attend the gathering, which took place every other year.

Ancient Mariners, Ancient Murderers

In Norway, Thorvald Asvaldsson was known as a bloodthirsty man and a law unto himself. He was a murderous warrior who relished thrusting his broadsword into the heart of an enemy. Because of that, Thorvald was banished from Norway and sailed westward to Iceland with his son, Erik the Red—so-called because of his red beard.

After Thorvald died, Erik followed in his father's footsteps. He had slaves called "thralls," as was common among the farmers of the time. When Erik's slaves caused a landslide in a neighbor's farm, Erik hired a "hitman," Eyiolf the Foul, to kill the thralls in revenge. Once Eyiolf accomplished his dastardly deed, Erik the Red slaughtered him. In the year 982, the Althing met and decided to exile Erik from Iceland. Like father, like son.

So, Erik the Red took his great Viking boat westward and eventually landed in Greenland. He favored the land and decided to gather a group of followers to sail back with him.

The Decline of Iceland

The country was divided into chieftaincies, but their power declined around the year 1200. By then, Iceland was a loose confederation.

In time, power struggles erupted among the leaders of the various segments of the country, resulting in chaos and violence. This was reflected in their literature of the time, as they told stories about a future drowning in warfare among the various clans and provinces. In the *Sagas of the Icelanders*, it is said that the soldiers carried "the heads of the slain and spears blood-besprinkled...and the air became bloodred through the heavens."

The Little Ice Age

In order to end the wars and clan conflicts, the strongest leader in Iceland, Snorri Sturluson, became a vassal of the king of Norway, Haakon IV, in 1218. Iceland was then placed under the direct control of Norway.

Sturluson's successors managed Iceland until a climactic crisis called the Little Ice Age occurred. Around 1380, temperatures plummeted. The ice sheet in the north extended. Winters became longer and colder, while the summers were short and chilly. This negatively affected Iceland's crops, their welfare, and, ultimately, their government. It became necessary during those times to import grain from Europe, as barley would no longer grow. Barley was their staple crop and was also used as animal feed, and the Little Ice Age caused an economic disaster because the importation of grain was so expensive.

To help alleviate the crisis, the Scandinavian countries—Denmark, Norway, and Sweden—united in order to support Iceland, as well as Greenland later on. Together they created what was called the Kalmar Union in 1397.

Greenland and the Norse Settlements

In 985 CE, the notorious Erik the Red took his hardy band from Iceland to Greenland. The waters were frigid and crashed violently against their wooden boats. The wind whipped within the fjords of Greenland, as they were full of hidden icebergs and extremely deep half-frozen waters. Out of Erik's fleet of 25, only fourteen boats managed to make the journey.

Erik and the people found on the western shore of Greenland small settlements of the late Dorset culture. The Inuit and Dorset mainly lived in northern and western Greenland, while the Norsemen settled in the southern and southwestern areas of the island.

Between 985 CE and the early 15th century, the Norse built manor houses. They traded furs, ivory, and even live polar bears to Norway and other parts of Europe. Other exotic goods of an artistic or productive nature were sold to Europe. Researchers have even found evidence that expensive articles like stained glass were imported.

Survival in Greenland

The people living in Greenland initially engaged in agriculture, but it was never as vigorous as it was in Iceland. The Inuit and Dorset in the north gradually declined due to soil erosion, which impacted agriculture. Some fishing did remain, but the ice sheets caused the migration of fish. Even seals and walruses weren't plentiful due to the expanding ice shelf and glacial expansion. Archeologists who have studied the northwestern regions of Greenland indicate that the Dorset and Inuit migrated southward and met up with the Norsemen.

There was some limited trade between the two cultures, but conflicts arose. The Inuit sometimes kidnapped the Norwegian children and made slaves of them. On occasion, the Inuit raided Norse villages.

In the south and southwestern regions, the Norsemen were able to trade ivory with Europe, but the declining prices of ivory on the mainland caused impoverishment in those economic sectors. The farmers were also affected by the overall soil erosion and deforestation that occurred as lumbering increased. Many turned to hunting. Caribou became the food of choice, and they chased the herds across the frozen land.

Unfortunately, the Norsemen had little experience in hunting. Their techniques were far less effective than those of the Inuit, who were able to eke out a living in the north, at least for a while.

Pastoralism became necessary for the people of Greenland, and they raised cows and pigs initially. They had to resort to raising sheep and goats later on when they realized there was insufficient fodder for the animals to survive.

Many learned to survive by hunting seal and sea mammals. In fact, their diet changed from meat to seafood as a result. However, the Norsemen were inexperienced in kayak navigation and were also far less effective in these matters than their northern neighbors, the Inuit.

The Disappearance of the Norsemen

In 1408, a Norseman named Thorstein Olafsson married Sigrid Bjornsdottir, after which they sent letters relating the news to their relatives in Norway. The couple had arrived there accidentally after being thrown off course on their way to Iceland. Reportedly, they settled there but later moved to Iceland. Those letters are thought to be the last known written records of the Norse in Greenland.

There were a few other written records during that period, but the Norse settlements seemed to have suddenly disappeared. One of the causes for the reduction in Greenland's population is that the Norsemen, who were unskilled at walrus and seal hunting, were killed in the many storms that took place on the seas. One of the theories is related to the Little Ice Age of 1380, as the effects of this event dragged on for many years. The main theories that prevail today indicate that a large number of the Norse settlers starved to death, causing the people to look elsewhere to settle, or that the settlers intermarried with the Inuit and migrated with them. However, no one knows for sure what happened to the Norse in Greenland.

Political Status

Because Greenland is frozen most of the time, these lands are virtually inaccessible. The population was and still is very sparse. From the 17th until the 20th century, Greenland was a part of Denmark and Norway. After the Napoleonic Wars and the Treaty of Kiel of 1814, Greenland was in the possession of Denmark.

Denmark was mostly interested in Greenland as a trading partner. Greenland was a site for scientific and geographical exploration, and many hardy Arctic adventurers, such as William Scoresby of England, Knud Rasmussen of Greenland, and Robert Peary of the United States, tried their luck in exploring the vast territory.

By virtue of Robert Peary's claim to the northern areas of Greenland, the United States claimed that area as a colony in 1909. However, in 1917, the United States exchanged it to Denmark for the possession of the islands of St. Croix, St. Thomas, and St. John.

World War II

In 1940, Denmark was invaded by Nazi Germany, severing its ties to Greenland. Between 1941 and 1945, the US occupied Greenland in order to protect it against invasions by Germany.

Before this point in time, Greenland was a very isolated country. Although it traded with Denmark, it didn't have much contact with the rest of the world. In 1950, Greenland made its first moves to become something more. With Denmark's approval, Greenland became a modern welfare state.

Home Rule of Greenland

In 1953, Greenland, which was still a part of Denmark, accepted the Danish Constitution. With this move, Greenland was no longer a colony; instead, it was on equal footing with Denmark. However, Denmark became increasingly invested in making sure Greenland was Danish. The Danish language was used in official matters and taught in schools, and many Greenlanders had to go to Denmark to complete their higher education. These steps made Greenlanders lose their cultural identity, and in the 1970s, they had had enough. In 1979, Denmark granted Greenland home rule. This gave the Greenlanders some autonomy, although Denmark still controlled most of the government, including security and foreign relations.

A major step toward Greenlandic independence happened not too long ago. In 2008, the Greenlandic self-government referendum was passed, which expanded home rule and gave Greenlanders more of a say in their government. A year later, another act was passed that made the official language of Greenland Greenlandic. This act also gave Greenlanders the right to declare full independence. As of writing this book, though, Greenland is still a part of Denmark.

Chapter 10 – The European Colonization of North America, 1492–1733

The Italian explorer John Cabot was sent by King Henry VII of England in 1497 to search for the Northwest Passage. After the journeys of Christopher Columbus, Europeans came to realize that the Americas lay between Europe and the Far East. However, they still believed there was some direct route that they could take to reach China and India by sailing westward. Explorers searched for centuries to find this mythical passage until one such passage was discovered in 1850, although, at the time, it was covered in ice and impossible to cross with ships. This route would take explorers west from Europe across the northern Atlantic Ocean, through the Arctic Ocean, and across the Pacific to the Far East.

Europeans Seek to Create Colonies

Christopher Columbus used to be lauded as the discoverer of the Americas, but historical research has proven that claim to not be true. Leif Eriksson, the son of Erik the Red, is actually the first known European to step on North American shores (excluding Greenland, which his father settled). Leif settled an area known as land, which is thought to have encompassed the eastern area of anada, around the Gulf of Saint Lawrence. Christopher Columbus, however, can be lauded as the man to bring large-scale colonization to the Americas. He landed on the island of what he called San Salvador, which is today located in the Bahamas, on October 12th, 1492. He thought he was in the Indies (known as the East Indies today), which is why he referred to the native peoples he encountered as *Indios*.

It wasn't until the Florentine merchant Amerigo Vespucci traveled to what is now Brazil in 1501 that Europeans began to realize that they had found something other than India. Vespucci is thought to be the first to realize this, calling the new land the "New World." His name, Amerigo, might seem similar to the name America, and for a good reason. By 1532, mapmakers had attached his name to the newly discovered continents. Some believe that Columbus knew he was on a different continent, but there has been no real conclusive proof to support the theory.

Vasco Núñez de Balboa, a Spaniard, helped support Vespucci's theory when he crossed Mesoamerica and found the Pacific Ocean in 1513. He is credited with being the first European to have seen the Pacific Ocean from the shores of the New World. In 1519, Portuguese Ferdinand Magellan organized a Spanish expedition to the East Indies, which would ultimately result in the first circumnavigation of the earth, although Magellan would not live to see it come to fruition. He and his crew sailed from England, crossed the Atlantic Ocean, went around South America, then crossed the Pacific Ocean to head to Asia. After sailing on the Pacific for months, and encountering many setbacks, Magellan and his surviving crew landed in the Philippines, which was where Magellan died after trying to forcibly convert the natives to Christianity. Juan Sebastián Elcano took over command and finished what Magellan had started. This journey proved, without doubt, that the newly discovered lands of the New World were not a part of India.

After Columbus's major discovery, another discovery took place, farther north. In 1497, Cabot landed in Newfoundland or Nova Scotia (historians are not sure where he exactly landed) and claimed the land for England. The Portuguese lost interest in this area when the opportunity to colonize South America arose. Since they concentrated their primary focus on Brazil, their fishing villages in the north were abandoned.

In 1534, Jacques Cartier "won" the rights to settle Canada for the French when he planted a cross overlooking the picturesque Gaspé Bay. The Gaspé Peninsula extends in a northeastern direction into the Gulf of St Lawrence. Topologically, it is made of up undulating slopes and depressions, in which fishing villages were eventually built. This was the beginning of what is known as New France, which, at its peak, included five large colonies. By 1712, New France extended from mideastern Canada to the southern tip of the Hudson Bay all the way south to the Port of New Orleans in Louisiana.

There were many "firsts" during this period of time, which is known as the Age of Discovery. We will hit upon one more before discussing some of the important colonies that were founded in the New World. In 1513, an explorer named Juan Ponce de León sighted a semi-tropical peninsula he called "Florida," which means "full of flowers." It was a rich land with luscious foliage and fruit. It has been rumored that he came there seeking the Fountain of Youth, a fabled body of water that is believed to give long life to whomever drinks or bathes in it. However, there is no clear evidence that Ponce de León was actually looking for the fountain. He makes no mention of it in his journals, and the first time it was brought up was after his death and by an author who may have done so for political reasons.

Florida was subject to further expeditions by European explorers, such as Spanish Pánfilo de Narváez in 1528, Spanish Hernando de Soto in 1539, French Rene Goulaine de Laudonnière in 1564, and Spanish Pedro Menéndez, who founded the oldest continually inhabited European settlement in the United States—St. Augustine—in 1565.

As one can piece together by now, the European countries of Spain, Britain, Portugal, and France fought to gain control of the New World. While the exploration of the New World opened up new possibilities, especially in the area of trade, it also inflicted numerous problems, problems that are still felt today. The diseases introduced by the Europeans to the native peoples of the New World devastated their populations, as they had no built-up immunity to them. Wars, conquests, and enslavement, in addition to disease, forced some cultures in North, South, and Central America to go entirely extinct.

The Thirteen Eastern Seaboard Colonies

The Lost Colony of Roanoke

The first attempt to establish a permanent English settlement occurred on Roanoke Island, located off the coast of today's North Carolina, in the late 1500s. Sir Walter Raleigh was determined to pave the way for English dominance in the New World, but both of his attempts to do so on the island failed. The colony of Roanoke is perhaps best known for the mysterious disappearance of its colonists. Many theories have been proposed as to what happened to them, with the most popular being that the natives killed them all or that the colonists integrated into Native American tribes.

Life at Jamestown, Virginia

In 1607, the London Company, a mercantile company created by King James I to establish settlements in the New World, established the first permanent English settlement in the Americas. This was Jamestown, located in the present state of Virginia.

Life was very difficult for the colonists, and food was scarce. In the winter of 1609/10, the colonists stared death in the face, and some had to resort to eating each other just to survive. And survive they did, as the colony began to grow soon after.

Initially, the people got along with the Native Americans in the region, namely the Powhatans. However, it did not last, and the First Anglo-Powhatan War ensued, which lasted from 1610 to 1614. The war ended with the capture of the Powhatan chief's daughter, Matoaka, better known as Pocahontas. She married John Rolfe, an enterprising man who was the first to successfully grow tobacco in Virginia. Tobacco became the colony's most popular crop, and it was traded throughout Europe. Due to the demand for the product, slaves were brought to the Americas to work in the fields.

Over time, more English settled there, and Virginia became a flourishing colony.

Massachusetts

In 1620, a group of people objected to some of the tenets of the Church of England, which was the prominent religion there. These people, who called themselves Pilgrims, officially separated from the Church of England, and to achieve religious freedom, they sailed to the New World aboard the *Mayflower.*

These Pilgrims reached the eastern tip of present-day Massachusetts. They called their settlement Plymouth.

Shortly afterward, another group of people seeking religious freedom arrived. These were the Puritans, and they weren't exactly separatists like their neighbors. Instead, they believed the Church of England needed to be purged of its many Roman Catholic practices. The founding of the Massachusetts Bay Colony took place in 1628, and it was founded by the Massachusetts Bay Company, which had a charter from the English king to settle there.

Their relations with the native tribes in the area, which included the Pequots and Nipmucks, among others, were initially very good. However, over time, tensions rose between the native populace and the Europeans, leading to conflicts like the Pequot War and King Philip's War.

New Hampshire

New Hampshire was settled as early as 1623 by the English, who took advantage of the rivers and bays to create fisheries. In 1638, John Wheelwright, a prominent Puritan preacher who had been banished from Massachusetts for supporting his sister-in-law, Anne Hutchinson, founded Exeter. This settlement became a safe haven for those seeking relief from the Puritan rule.

New Hampshire lacked a strong central government and relied upon the help of the Massachusetts Bay Colony for some time. It wasn't until 1679 that the Province of New Hampshire was established.

Maryland

In 1632, King Charles issued a charter for Maryland, which he intended to be a refuge for English Catholics. The land would not be permanently inhabited until two years later. As in other colonies, the new settlers of Maryland got along with the Native Americans well. They taught the colonists how to grow corn and beans and how to hunt for clams and oysters. And, as in other colonies, these peaceful relations eventually grew into hostile ones.

In 1649, the government of Maryland passed the Toleration Act, which permitted religious tolerance for all Christians. However, the act also called for the deaths of those who did not believe in the divinity of Jesus Christ.

Connecticut

In 1636, colonists, under the leadership of John Haynes and Thomas Hooker, moved westward out of Massachusetts and essentially founded the colony of Connecticut.

Rhode Island

The rigid Puritan rule in Massachusetts led to the exile of a Puritan theologian named Roger Williams, who left the colony in 1636 and established a new colony just north of Massachusetts, which he called Providence Plantation. He and the colonists there established a policy of freedom of religion.

Williams purchased the land from two chiefs of the Narragansetts, and as such, the Rhode Islanders had a mutually beneficial relationship with the tribes in the area. Over time, other colonies began to pop up in the surrounding areas, and Williams was able to unite them all with a charter, which was granted in 1663.

Delaware

The region of Delaware had been inhabited by other Europeans before the British came to own it. Originally, the land was inhabited by the Lenape and the Assateague tribes, an Algonquian-speaking people. In 1609, the Dutch discovered Delaware, and in the following years, more mapping was done of the region. In 1629, the Dutch were ready to buy the area from the Native Americans, and the first colony was built in 1631. However, due to a misunderstanding between the Native Americans, the colony was quickly abandoned after the colonists were attacked, which resulted in 28 deaths.

The first permanent settlement of Delaware would not be the Dutch but rather the Swedes. In 1638, New Sweden was established, and they remained firmly in control for about a decade. However, the Dutch, not viewing the Swedish settlement as legitimate, came back to retrieve what they believed was rightfully theirs. Fighting ensued in the early 1650s, and by 1655, the Dutch had won. They wouldn't get to enjoy their hard-won victory for too long, though. Once the British captured New Amsterdam, the seat of New Netherland (which will be discussed more in-depth below) in 1664, it was only a matter of time before they moved onto capturing Delaware.

The Carolinas

The original charter for this colony was issued in 1629, but it was deemed invalid, mainly for political reasons, and it wasn't until 1663 that the Province of Carolina was actually formed.

In 1670, King Charles II commissioned a group of English noblemen to establish a city that they called Charles Town (today's Charleston). More settlers followed them, and they discovered that the soil in this area was fertile and the growing season long, making it ideal for farming.

In 1712, the Province of Carolina was broken into two, with the creation of the colonies of North and South Carolina.

New Netherland

In 1621, while Massachusetts was being settled, the Dutch established their own colony of New Netherland. It reached from Albany, New York, to Delaware, although it also claimed parts of what are now New Jersey, Connecticut, Pennsylvania, and Maryland.

Peter Stuyvesant was the feisty Dutchman who controlled New Netherland from 1647 to 1664. Britain wanted a contiguous set of colonies, running from Massachusetts to the Carolinas. Therefore, they challenged the Dutch and threatened hostility. In 1664, England sent a fleet of ships to the harbor of New Amsterdam. Stuyvesant refused to capitulate and wanted to go to war over it. However, the Dutch colonists refused to back him up.

So, without firing a shot, New Netherland surrendered, and it became known as the Province of New York. Following that, the duke of York granted the land south of New York to the east of the Delaware River to two English nobles. This was called New Jersey.

Sadly, the English were not kind to the Dutch living there. Pillaging and looting took place along the Delaware River, and many Dutch were sold into slavery. The Second Anglo-Dutch War, which took place between 1665 and 1667, did not help to ease the tensions between the two great nations. By 1673, New Netherland was in the hands of the Dutch once more.

But it would not stay there for long. The Third Anglo-Dutch War, which took place between 1672 and 1674, caused the Dutch Republic to go bankrupt, and although the Dutch won the war, they realized they didn't have the resources to protect their holdings in the New World and ceded it to the English in the resulting peace treaty.

Pennsylvania

William Penn was the son of an admiral, although he himself did not pursue a military career and instead became a writer. In 1682, Penn was granted a large plot of land west of the Delaware River as a payment for a debt the king owed his father. Since Penn was a member of the Quaker religion, which was not tolerated in England very well, he ensured that his colony encouraged religious freedom. Penn and his followers founded Philadelphia, which is Greek for "brotherly love."

Georgia

England permitted James Oglethorpe to lay claim to the territory that was south of the Carolinas in 1732. One of the purposes of claiming this colony for England was to prevent the further spread of Spanish colonies in North America, as just below that region was Florida, which Spain owned. Colonists didn't actually occupy the territory until about a year later.

Government

In the beginning, not all of the colonies were overseen by Britain. In fact, in 1680, only Virginia was a royal colony. Over time, each of the aforementioned colonies would become a part of Britain. These colonies were overseen by royal governors, who were appointed by the British Parliament.

Trade

The Thirteen Colonies conducted trade with England. The colonies exported iron, grain, cattle, tobacco, tar, pitch, rice, and indigo. England exported manufactured goods to America like clothing, china, glass, household items, and other products that couldn't be manufactured in the colonies. Smugglers grew in popularity in order to trade with other nations, which would be one of the many factors that led to the American Revolution.

New France

While the English were establishing colonies along the Eastern seaboard, France controlled Quebec in current-day Canada and swept down into the huge territory known as the Ohio Valley. From there, it went all the way down to the Gulf of Mexico. In 1605 and onward, France expanded its settlements in the Midwest, and in 1650, France had more territory in North America than England. However, they had fewer settlements.

Quebec

The first official settlement in Canada was founded by Samuel de Champlain in 1608. It was built to be a trading post, as fur trading was very lucrative in northern North America. The majority of the population in and around Quebec, excluding the natives who made it their home, namely the Innu and Algonquins, was French, and the people who lived there practiced French customs. The vernacular language was French, and most of the people who live in today's Quebec City speak it.

Trade

The primary occupation of the French in North America was fur trading. They also established close relationships with the native tribes, particularly the Algonquian-speaking peoples and the Hurons of the Midwest.

Chapter 11 – North American Conflicts, Including America's War for Independence, 1754–1783

The French and Indian War, 1754-1763

The French occupation of the Ohio Valley blocked the western expansion of British America. Although France did not have nearly as many settlements as the British, they had built a series of fortresses in that region, leading all the way up to Lake Erie. It should be noted that while many Americans view the French and Indian War as a separate conflict, others see the war as being a part of the American theater of the broader Seven Years' War, which lasted from 1756 to 1763.

The disagreement originally started over who controlled a certain region, namely the Forks of Ohio. Violence finally erupted in 1754 when a Virginia militia under future president George Washington and some Native American allies ambushed the French.

In 1755, General Edward Braddock of the British Army arrived to help plan a coordinated attack against the French. However, he was defeated by the French and died soon after. Fortunes changed, though, when William Pitt, a member of the British Cabinet, persuaded the colonists to provide more troops and sent more experienced leaders from England to lead them.

General James Wolfe, among others, led troops that captured the fort in Louisbourg, located in Novia Scotia, in 1758. The loss of this fort was catastrophic for the British as they no longer had a source of protection along the Saint Lawrence River. Over a year later, Wolfe would use Louisbourg to launch his attack on Quebec. Wolfe died in the battle, but the British victory only continued to apply the pressure on the French. The French continued to put up a fight, but by 1760, the main fighting had concluded.

The conflict was officially over in 1763 with the Treaty of Paris, which also signaled the end of the Seven Years' War. As a result of the treaty, France surrendered their holdings east of the Mississippi River. They still retained the western half of Louisiana, which included the Port of New Orleans, but they handed it over to Spain in a secret treaty that was signed a year before. Spain also gave up eastern Florida to the British as well.

The French did, however, retain the rights to fish off Newfoundland and the islands of Saint Pierre and Miquelon. During this time, they continued to foster relationships with the Native American tribes in Canada.

England's Control

In the 1660s, England passed the first of the Navigation Acts, which required that all goods exported from the New World be sold through them. The same held true for imports from countries other than England. Over time, more acts would be passed, and for the most part, they were followed. That is until the Molasses Act of 1733, in which Britain imposed an outrageous tax on imports of molasses that came from non-English colonies, mainly the French

West Indies. Smuggling became rampant, and the law wasn't really obeyed. It was later renewed as a part of the Sugar Act of 1764, which the British expected the colonists to follow since they halved the tax in half. However, due to the expenses incurred from supporting the British during the Seven Years' War, the economies of the colonies were floundering, and the cracks between the colonies and Britain began to solidify.

In 1765 and 1767, England passed the Stamp Act and the Townsend Acts, respectively, which placed even more financial burdens on the colonists. More taxes were charged, particularly on tea, their favorite beverage. Things came to a head in 1770 with the Boston massacre, in which a group of British soldiers was antagonized by the colonists, eventually leading to the deaths of five colonists when one of the soldiers shot into the crowd.

In 1773, colonial resistance movements started to form. It was during this year that the famous Boston Tea Party took place, in which colonists, dressed as Mohawk warriors, dumped 342 chests of tea into the waters of Boston Harbor. In 1774, the Intolerable Acts were passed, which restricted the rights of the colonists to meet, closed Boston Harbor, and allowed British soldiers to room in civilians' houses, among other harsh acts. The First Continental Congress met the same year and agreed to boycott British goods. Local militias began to be trained, and in February 1775, Britain declared Massachusetts to be in a state of rebellion.

The American Revolution 1775–1783

A leader arose from Virginia by the name of George Washington. He became the commander in chief of the Continental Army in June 1775 (after the Battles of Lexington and Concord). The army was poorly supplied at the beginning, but their intense motivation and knowledge of the land helped make up for what they lacked in resources.

Battles of Lexington and Concord

In the spring of 1775, the British left the confines of Boston and marched through the Massachusetts Bay Colony in search of weapons stored in armories. They headed for the town of Concord, where there was a large depot. Unknown to the British, the weapons there and in other armories in Massachusetts had been hidden.

They marched through the town of Lexington on their way, and a shot rang out. According to Ralph Waldo Emerson, it was "the shot heard 'round the world." The British then fired a volley of shots. The Patriots pulled back but followed the British stealthily. The British regiments searched Concord and the countryside, destroying what they could find. When the British marched back to Boston, the Patriots attacked once more, putting the British under heavy fire.

In the spring of 1776, the Continental Army expelled the British from Boston, who regrouped in Nova Scotia.

Formation of "States"

The Battle of Bunker Hill in 1775 was an important moment in the war. Although the British technically won it, it came at a heavy loss, and the Americans now knew they could stand up to the British Army. The British took a more cautious approach in the war from this point on, which ended up helping the Americans. After the Battle of Bunker Hill, the Patriots found themselves in control of Massachusetts. The colonies declared themselves to be independent states and began developing their own constitutions, which took place between 1775 and 1776. They also set up their own state governments. On July 4th, 1776, the Americans declared their independence from the British with the Declaration of Independence, which was mostly written by Virginia statesman Thomas Jefferson. In 1781, the Articles of Confederation were ratified, which served as the law of the new land.

Short Summary of the Actions of the War (1776–1781)

Late in the summer of 1776, the English, under General William Howe, arrived in New York Harbor and seized the city, burning much of it.

Washington marched his troops through eastern Pennsylvania. He and his troops then surprised the British at their winter headquarters in Trenton, defeating them in late December. Following that, they trounced them at Princeton in early 1777.

The British troops swept down from the Hudson Valley under General John Burgoyne to meet up with some of Howe's troops, who planned to meet up and attack the Patriots at Albany. The plan failed, but they were confronted by the Patriots at Saratoga, New York, in September 1777. The British were badly defeated in the battle. Many see this as the turning point in the war.

Following that astounding victory, France officially became an ally. Marquis de Lafayette led fleets of vessels into the Atlantic, while French ground troops landed to help the Americans. In 1778, Britain began to focus on the southern states and did very well, taking Charleston in 1780. During the summer of 1781, the French and American forces met up and began their drive south.

Lieutenant General Charles Cornwallis commanded the contingent of British troops in Virginia, and the two sides waged a bloody land and sea battle at Yorktown, Virginia, beginning in late September 1781. With the British forces completely surrounded, they were forced to surrender in mid-October.

The Treaty of Paris

When the Treaty of Paris was signed in 1783, a boundary was delineated between the independent colonies and the British lands north of there in Canada. Britain gave up its claims to the colonies and recognized the independence of the new United States.

The war left the new country unstable and in severe debt. These were problems that the government would have to quickly address, as the country needed to find its place in a world that was constantly seized by conflicts.

US Constitution

After the war, the states realized that their new government was weak and that the structure had to be modified.

From July until September 1787, a group of delegates held intensive sessions and drew up the US Constitution, which replaced the Articles of Confederation. It was sent to the states and was ratified in 1788, although it would not be ratified by all the states until 1790.

The Constitution remains the law of the land in the United States to this day, and it defines the separation of government and the role of state governments. The Constitution also consists of amendments, with the first ten being known as the Bill of Rights, which guarantees liberties and freedoms to the people. Over time, other amendments were added, which mostly granted additional rights to the people living in the US.

George Washington and His Cabinet

In early 1789, George Washington was unanimously elected as the first president of the United States. He had a Cabinet of five officers, with the more prominent names being Alexander Hamilton as secretary of the treasury, Thomas Jefferson as secretary of the state, and John Jay as the chief justice.

George Washington would do much to secure the new country's safety, including his refusal to aid the French during their own revolution, despite the fact they had assisted the US with theirs. The danger was just too great for the fledging country, and Washington knew they wouldn't be able to fight a war so far away and come out successful. Although he could have easily run for more than two terms, he chose not to, as he did not want the country to set a precedent that a tyrant would be able to abuse. Washington is often viewed as one of the greatest presidents in United States history.

Chapter 12 – North America: Mexico and Canada, 1821–1982

The Viceroyalty of New Spain in North America

One of the many indigenous peoples of Mexico were the Aztecs. In 1519, the once-powerful empire was defeated by the mighty armored forces of the Spanish conquistadors and their native allies led by Hernán Cortés. As foretold by their ancient god Huitzilopochtli, the land of Mexica-Tenochtitlan would be made anew. In an Aztec poem, Huitzilopochtli boldly asks, "Who could conquer Tenochtitlan? Who could shake the foundation of heaven?" The answer had arrived. This would no longer be Mexica-Tenochtitlan; instead, it would become New Spain.

By 1783, Mexico was under the management of the Viceroyalty of New Spain. However, the Spanish claims were grandiose. The Spaniards claimed that they possessed the modern-day American states of New Mexico, Texas, Arizona, Colorado, Utah, Arizona, Florida, and Louisiana. These huge territories were separated into large provinces, each with its own governmental body. New Spain lasted until 1821, the year when Mexico became independent.

The Mexican War of Independence, 1810–1821

In 1808, Charles IV, the king of Spain, was deposed by Napoleon Bonaparte's forces. Napoleon then put his brother, Joseph, in charge of the Spanish colonies, which included the Viceroyalty of New Spain. The people of the Mexican territories, most of whom were Criollos, people who were born in South America but had Spanish blood, craved independence from Spain and took advantage of the chaos in Europe.

José de Iturrigaray, the viceroy of New Spain from 1803 to 1808, was deposed during a coup, and Pedro de Garibay was named the new viceroy. De Garibay and those who put him in power were in favor of total independence from Spain.

The Cry of Dolores: Hidalgo's Revolt

In the very small city of Dolores, a courageous priest by the name of Miguel Hidalgo marched across Mexico, gathering an army of nearly 100,000 people, mostly farmers. They had been economically crippled by the prohibition of the growing of olives and grapes, which only made Spain wealthier as they grew those crops themselves.

Since they weren't military men, they were poorly armed, but they presented the Spanish-born elites and the Criollos with a challenge. In January 1811, the Battle of Calderón Bridge was fought in west-central Mexico, and it was a literal bloodbath. Six thousand well-trained and well-armed Spanish soldiers nearly wiped the rebels out. Hidalgo and his other military leaders fled but were later captured, tried, and then either shot or imprisoned.

Insurgency under Morelos and Rayón

The struggle did not end with Hidalgo's death. The rebels formed under two priests, José María Morelos and Ignacio López Rayón.

In the Battle of Zacatecas in April 1811, López Rayón defeated the Spanish forces and gained possession of the town. Zacatecas was an industrial city that manufactured artillery and weapons, which was a big win for the rebels. At the Battle of El Maguey that May, the rebels lost to the forces of the Spanish under General Miguel Emparan but inflicted much damage. Under the cover of gun smoke, the rebels were able to retreat, blinding Emparan and his soldiers who moved in a different direction. The Spanish loyalist forces again defeated the Mexican rebels at the Battle of Zitácuaro.

In September 1813, Morelos called together representatives of the provinces the rebels controlled to further unite their efforts, which included Rayón. The Congress of Chilpancingo clarified their goals and declared that "America is free and independent from Spain." Also, it forbade slavery and abolished the old social castes based on heritage.

After the Congress had met, Morelos began a new set of campaigns, which led to utter disaster. Félix María Calleja del Rey, the viceroy of New Spain and the leader of the Spanish royalist forces at the time, captured Morelos in 1815. Morelos was charged with treason and was executed in the name of Spain.

Vicente Ramón Guerrero Saldana picked up the torch from there and organized a new revolutionary army. He was a mestizo, that is a man of mixed blood. Although his parents were loyalists, Guerrero was not. He was trained as a militiaman and was a skilled gunsmith, so he had a lot of experience compared to other revolutionaries.

Insurgency under Vicente Guerrero

Guerrero joined up with a homegrown guerilla force under Guadalupe Victoria. In the meantime, one of Guerrero's units under Martín Javier Mina was captured by the royalists in 1817. Because of that capture, the viceroy thought that Spain had effectively won the war, and as a gesture to inspire loyalty to Spain, he extended amnesty to the rebels.

Many surrendered their weapons and stood behind the viceroy. Thus, the war became a stalemate until 1820. During this period of time, the Criollos lost interest in the war and returned to their trade. The rebels were smaller in numbers, but they continued their resistance. During those three years, they conducted sporadic raids on the Spanish using guerilla tactics, and they often caught the more disciplined Spanish troops off balance.

What's more, back in Europe, Napoleon had been defeated, and the government had been restored to King Ferdinand VII. Once King Ferdinand was in power, he cut the pay of the soldiers in New Spain. The Spanish soldiers attempted to get financial support from the residents in order to continue their campaigns. The effort was nearly hopeless, so the Spanish soldiers instead confiscated property from the locals and started running their haciendas. As a result, many of them became involved in mercantilism.

In 1820, Spanish then sent a powerful general, Agustín de Iturbide, to go up against Guerrero. However, Guerrero prevailed. This raised the morale of the Mexicans to the point that even the Catholic clergy urged revolution. In those days, religious prelates were highly politicized and had the command of the minds and hearts of the people. Guerrero was a persuasive leader, which resulted in attaining the loyalty of his former enemy, Agustín de Iturbide, who had his troops join up with Guerrero.

In February 1821, the two leaders drafted the Plan of Iguala. It stated that the future country would be a constitutional monarchy under Mexican leadership. Because of the support of the Church, it stipulated that its official religion was Roman Catholicism. The plan made three guarantees to the people: independence, the dominance of Catholicism, and social equality.

Not everyone agreed with the plan, but over time, Guerrero and Iturbide were able to convince the common people and even those fighting for the royalists to see their side of things. By August 1821, nearly the whole country supported the Iguala Plan, and on August 24th, the Treaty of Córdoba ended the war. Mexico was now a free and independent country. Spain did not recognize this, though, and it would later attempt to take Mexico again. However, the Mexicans rejoiced in their freedom, and on September 27th, 1821, Iturbide officially declared the independence of the Mexican Empire. Its southern border lay at the Mexican provinces of Oaxaca, Veracruz, and Yucatan. Its northern border did include some territories in the modern-day United States, including California, Nevada, New Mexico, Utah, western Arizona, western Colorado, and Texas.

Mexican-American War

Although this took place after Mexico's independence movement, it is interesting to take a look at this war because it set the modern-day borders of the United States and Mexico. After Mexico's War of Independence, the United States was looking toward expanding its western border right up to the Pacific Ocean. To help achieve that, America annexed Texas in 1845. The war for independence had already drained Mexico of its resources, personnel, and weapons. What's more, it wasn't yet a unified country with a sense of nationalism. When Mexican President Santa Anna requested supplies from the states, only seven of nineteen states sent materials and supplies for the war effort. Politics played a divisive role in separating the military from the government in charge of it.

The formidable Major-General Zachary Taylor, who would one day be the president of the United States, headed up the American forces, while President Santa Anna led the Mexican units.

In his memoirs, Ulysses S. Grant, a future general and president of the United States, wrote, "The Mexican Army of that day was hardly an organization. The private soldier was picked from the lower class of the inhabitants when wanted; his consent was not asked; he was poorly clothed, and worse fed, and seldom paid." Although these statements seem harsh, they were, for the most part, true. Just as Mexico was not united, neither was its army. Desertion was common, and the Mexicans used poor firearms compared to the US soldiers.

The war was fought on many fronts, including modern-day New Mexico, Arizona, Texas, California, along the Pacific Coast, in northeastern and northwestern Mexico, on the Yucatan Peninsula, and even Mexico City. However, it should be noted that these territories belonged to Mexico at the time. The territory of Texas was in dispute, although Mexico viewed it as belonging to them.

In California, General José Castro gathered up his Mexican forces to defend the territory. In the meantime, an American band of settlers engaged in what is known as the Bear Flag Revolt in June 1846. They captured the Mexican post at Sonoma, which was undefended. After hearing that Castro was planning an attack, US Army Captain John Fremont and his troops headed toward Sonoma, and after their victory, they absorbed this group into their own.

In the territory of Nuevo Mexico, which included the current states of New Mexico and Arizona, General Stephen Kearny and his troops entered the city of Santa Fe in August 1846, claiming it for the United States without a shot being fired. Kearney set up a civilian government before heading to Alta California (the upper region of the California territory).

In the San Francisco Bay, the battleship USS *Portsmouth* disembarked its troops under Commodore Robert Stockton, and they marched to San Diego. The vigorous general Stephen Kearny marched his forces across the Sonoran Desert in New Mexico and met up with Stockton's men. They then moved north toward Los Angeles.

To protect his men, who were running low on supplies, General José María Flores moved away from the Los Angeles garrison and reconnoitered at the San Gabriel bluff. There, he was confronted with the combined troops of Commodore Stockton and General Kearny. After a two-hour battle at the San Gabriel River, they defeated Flores and his men. They then marched into Los Angeles, with the Mexicans offering no resistance.

In 1848, the Treaty of Guadalupe Hidalgo was signed. It granted the United States a huge chunk of Mexican territory. Mexico was paid $15 million for this, and its debt of $3.25 million was also assumed by America. Any Mexican living in the ceded territories was granted US citizenship.

Canada

To refresh, the Treaty of Paris, signed in 1763, gave Britain the territories in Canada, except for a few spots where the French claimed fishing rights. In the beginning, the British tried to tamper down the influence of the French, including the restriction of religion. For instance, in Quebec, nearly 70,000 French could not vote due to their Roman Catholic faith.

The Haldimand Proclamation

In 1784, the British awarded a generous land grant to the Iroquois, who had helped them during the American Revolution. However, disputes eventually arose over the land. As time went by, the area became more heavily settled by white men, and the natives decided to move west. Many of the tribes along the US-Canadian border were allowed free passage. They were mostly trappers and hunters.

Nootka Crisis

During the very early exploration of the North American continent, Spain and France had an active trade with the French fur trappers in the area of Nootka, located in the Pacific Northwest. When the veteran explorer James Cook mapped out the area, Great Britain established its own trade routes and did a hefty business with China. In 1789, Spain sent ships over there to defend their own trading rights and confiscated some of the British ships in the region. America also sent ships there, although it was a brand-new nation without much to offer. The French king interfered, backing Spain's right to the land. The three countries belligerently defended their claims there. Despite mobilizing their army, the French decided not to engage in war. So, Spain decided to seek a more diplomatic solution. Britain was permitted to have control of the area, but it would be open to both British and Spanish traders. This territory eventually became the province of British Columbia.

War of 1812

Although this event was covered above, it was a pivotal event in Canadian history, and as such, it will be briefly summarized here as well so readers can get the full picture of the history of the country. The British impressed American seamen frequently in order to increase their manpower during the Seven Years' War, which was being fought in Europe. They also blockaded American ports to prevent the shipment of supplies to their enemies. Because Canada lay so close to America, President James Madison, felt that Upper Canada (Ontario) was a viable target. Since Britain controlled Canada, an attack there would serve as a retaliatory move for the economic stress created by the blockade. Moreover, Upper Canada was inhabited by Americans who might be sympathetic to the American cause.

British Major General Isaac Brock knew that war was pending and built up a number of fortifications. The Americans attacked at Queenston Heights but were thwarted by Brock and his force of British regulars, Native Americans who had allied with Britain, and a force of black Canadians, known as the Coloured Corps. Unfortunately, Brock died in that battle.

The British troops confronted the American soldiers at York (present-day Toronto), but it didn't fall, and the British were forced to abandon the town. American ships sailed up the Niagara River and seized Fort George. British General John Vincent retreated from the fort and attacked the American forces at Stoney Creek. The battle was a bloody one, but the British were victorious. At Beaver Dams, the Kahnawake and Mohawk warriors trounced the Americans and took 600 of them as prisoners.

At the Battle of the Thames, the British lost perhaps their first major battle of the war, as their Shawnee patron, Tecumseh, was killed. This was a great loss because Tecumseh was able to unite many disparate tribes, and with his death, the alliance between the British and the Native Americans fell apart.

Eventually, both sides grew tired of the war, as neither side was making any particular headway. The Treaty of Ghent ended the war in 1815. Under the terms of the treaty, everything went back to the way it was before the war. The War of 1812 proved to the Americans that the annexation of Canada wasn't a feasible military objective, and it served to encourage the Canadians to bond together as a nation.

The Durham Report

In 1837, patriots Louis-Joseph Papineau in Lower Canada and William McKenzie of Upper Canada rebelled for the cause of freedom from England. The farmers, in particular, suffered many setbacks, and all the people wanted a responsible government that could handle revenue crises. Nether rebellion was ostensibly effective, but the protests and skirmishes continued for a year.

All of this drew the attention of John Lambton, Earl of Durham. He went to Canada to investigate and sized up the situation. Although his report stirred up controversy, Britain could see its wisdom because the British weren't aware of local needs.

The Durham Report promoted the creation of local and responsible governments. Many elites in Upper Canada rejected it, as they were the ones currently in power and did not want to upset the status quo. Despite their misgivings, the report eventually led to the unification of Upper and Lower Canada, along with the provinces of New Brunswick and Nova Scotia, in 1841.

Unification of Canada

In the 1860s, Canada wasn't a formal union; instead, it was a territory dotted with various British colonies. Although attempts had been made at uniting them into one, they had all failed. In 1864, another attempt was made with the Charlottetown Conference. They decided that New Brunswick, Novia Scotia, and Prince Edward Island would become one. The members also talked about what the government would be like and what their relationship with Britain would be.

Later that year, the Quebec Conference was held, which saw the inclusion of Newfoundland. In the conference, it was decided that Canada would have a strong central government, that provinces would have their own local governments, and that they would maintain ties with Britain. Many Canadians agreed with the proposal, but there were, of course, some who did not. British-Canadians were excited about the prospect of having a country that was uniform in British beliefs, but there were many French-Canadians who did not agree with such views.

In late 1866, the London Conference was held, during which the British government reviewed what the Quebec Conference had come up with. It was decided that Canada would become a British dominion, a semi-independent state. Queen Victoria bestowed her royal blessing upon the decision in March 1867.

Fortressing that effort, the British North America Act of 1867 solidified the dominion of Canada and established the various branches of government. The Constitution Act of 1867 laid the foundations for the Constitution of Canada and delineated departments of the administration as well as their respective powers, although it had to have approval from England.

Constitution of Canada

The British North America Act acted as Canada's constitution. It established an executive division with the British monarch as the chief executive, a legislature that consisted of the Senate and the House of Commons, and a criminal code. Each province had its own legislative, executive, and justice divisions. The executive tasks were carried out by the prime minister and by the executive governors of all the provinces.

Below that were departments that covered issues affecting all Canadians, such as civil rights, property rights, marriage, education, agriculture, pensions, and a division for dealing with affairs related to the indigenous peoples. Like in the United States, the natives lived on reservations.

There was another national division called works and undertakings. Because individual provinces ruled themselves independently, there were occasional projects that affected all of Canada, like a railroad or a dam. This came under the management of works and undertakings.

In 1982, a revised Constitution Act was passed, called the Canada Act. It eliminated the need for incessant British approval and empowered prime ministers and the legislature to make further changes to the Canadian Constitution as needed. Today, Canada is seen as an independent country, although it is still technically a part of the British Commonwealth.

Chapter 13 – Cuba and the West Indies

Cuba

Around 3100 BCE, Cuba and the islands surrounding it were inhabited by the Cayo Redondo and Guayabo Blanco. They were fishermen, hunters, and gatherers. In the 15th century, two migrant groups from the northern portions of South America, the Taíno and the Ciboney, migrated to Cuba. The local tribes intermarried and became part of the larger native group of the Arawaks, who originally came from Venezuela. DNA research also indicates that some of these migrants came from the Amazon River Basin. Some of these peoples settled the other islands of the Caribbean. In Cuba, most settled on the eastern side of the island. They grew maize, yucca, cotton, tobacco, and sweet potatoes.

Spanish Colonization of Cuba

The coast of Cuba was mapped by the Spanish navigator Sebastián de Ocampo in 1508, and in 1511, conquistador Diego Velázquez Cuéllar created the first Spanish settlement in Cuba at Baracoa. The conquistadors were cruel conquerors, and rather than placate the Taíno, who didn't want the Spaniards there and saw no incentive in having them stay, they rounded up the leaders of the Taíno rebellion and burned them alive. In 1514, they founded Havana. This was followed up by another brutal assault on the natives of Caonao, who hadn't offered any resistance. Instead, they offered the foreigners gifts. Nevertheless, they were butchered. The rest of the population was settled onto reservations, and many were enslaved. The Spanish also brought with them diseases hitherto unknown to the natives, and many perished from smallpox and measles.

During the 17th and 18th centuries, sugar plantations were founded. African slaves were imported by the thousands to work in the fields. By the 19th century, sugar was the primary crop in Cuba. Spain then manipulated the world market and became the main marketplace for sugar, which greatly enhanced the value of its trade routes. They also introduced watermills and more advanced techniques for refining and producing sugar by using furnaces and steam engines.

Spain did, however, pass trade regulations that lowered the prosperity of the sugar industry by attempting to monopolize it, forbidding foreign ships from buying sugar directly from Cuba.

Cuba was once a tropical island with luscious plants, but many had been torn down to allow for the growth of sugar plantations. The port cities were crowded with sloops and cargo ships anxious to conduct a brisk trade with the colonies in British America and overseas. Only the landowners and larger import-export offices received a decent income. Everyone else was engaged in menial work in the fields or labored in the counting houses of clerks and money changers.

The Path toward the Independence of Cuba

In 1607, the Spanish Empire created the Captaincy General of Cuba, as Spain had sought to protect and control the Caribbean area. The many movements for independence around the world showed Cuba that freedom could be theirs if they just took it. In 1809, Joaquín Infante, a member of the Cuban aristocracy, declared Cuba to be a sovereign state. He conspired to seize control of the island, but his insurrection was thwarted by Spain, and he was deported. In 1812, José Antonio Aponte, a mixed-race abolitionist, gained support from the many Cubans who detested slavery. His movement was also crushed by Spain, and Aponte was executed.

To help placate the rebels, the Spanish Constitution of 1812 was created, under which local representation was permitted in the governing council. However, once King Ferdinand VII was restored to the Spanish throne after Napoleon was exiled, he eliminated many of the liberal reforms in the Spanish Constitution.

In 1826, armed rebellions broke out in Cuba, which were led by people of different races. One by one, they were suppressed, and their leaders executed. The rebels wanted the abolition of slavery and the right to be represented in Spain. The British would soon end slavery in its colonies in 1833, and they attempted to pressure Spain to do the same. Spain resisted and resorted to cruel torture and executions to quell the various rebellions led by free blacks, mulattos, and even white intellectuals. In 1844, 300 blacks were tortured to death, 78 were executed, and 1,000 more were imprisoned or expelled.

In 1865, the wealthier Cubans demanded Cuban representation in the Spanish Parliament, judicial equality with the full-blooded Spaniards, freedom of the press (which had been silenced), and a ban on the slavery trade. None of these were met.

Cuba: The Ten Years' War

Despite the failure of these initial rebellions, Cuba was still determined to be independent. A strong leader rose from among the people: Carlos Manuel de Céspedes. He owned a sugar mill and had the widespread support of other wealthy landowners and natives. He stated, "Our aim is to throw off the Spanish yoke, and to establish a free and independent nation. When Cuba is free, it will have a constitutional government created in an enlightened manner."

On October 10th, 1868, Céspedes issued a cry of independence, freeing his slaves and inviting them to join others in the war against the Spanish. Initially, 12,000 rebels joined, and by October 13th, they had seized control of eight towns. Major General Máximo Gómez taught the Cubans some tactics they could employ to engage the Spanish forces, as most of the Cubans were ill-equipped and poorly trained.

The army conquered the city of Bayamo, then proceeded to the cities of Camagüey and Las Villas. Some of the western provinces, however, didn't support this war, including Havana. The rebel army faced some victories and defeats during the year, and many notable names rose up from the ranks, including Antonio Maceo Grajales and Federico Fernández Cavada.

In 1869, a constitutional assembly was formed in Camagüey. They separated the civilian government from the military, and two men served as the authors of the first constitution: General Ignacio Agramonte y Loynáz and Antonio Zambrana. The government was to be run by a House of Representatives under a president, the first of whom would be Céspedes.

The Spanish forces made an attempt to negotiate with the revolutionaries. They failed to reach an agreement, though, which greatly incensed the Spanish. They arrested leaders of insurgency groups and immediately executed them. Ships coming into port were searched for weapons, and if any were found, the entire crew and its passengers were executed. Male civilians were required to be on their plantations or at their homes. If anyone was found elsewhere, they were shot. Women who didn't stay at home were shipped off to labor camps.

Unwilling to give up easily, guerilla fighters continued the cause for independence, mainly fighting on the eastern side of the island. When Ignacio Agramonte, one of the commanders, was killed in May 1873, disagreements arose, and the Cuban Assembly replaced Céspedes with Salvador Cisneros. Shortly after that, Céspedes himself was killed in combat. In 1878, neither side was prevailing in the conflict, and both had grown tired of the fighting.

The war ended without a resolution. The Pact of Zanjón was signed, but it essentially was nothing more than a truce. It promised to grant more liberties to the Cubans, but by the following year, the Spanish had already returned to ruling with a more iron fist. By the end of the Ten Years' War, between 50,000 and 100,000 Cubans had been killed, and between 81,000 and 90,000 Spaniards had died, most due to illness.

Cuban War of Independence

In the year 1870, many Cuban exiles settled in and around the US state of Florida. They had closely followed the events in Cuba, and many of them wanted Spain to surrender its interest in the island nation. Cuba had suffered economically because of the war and the manipulation of financiers. There were virtually very few sugar mills that functioned at full capacity. Wealthy Cubans had their resources confiscated by the Spanish, along with their property. Among the exiles was the charismatic leader, José Martí, a political philosopher and poet. He inspired his countrymen to support independence in Cuba, and he was very much against the annexation of Cuba by the United States.

Martí and his followers, along with a group of Cuban exiles, gave impetus to a number of insurrections in Cuba, in cities like Santiago, Guantánamo, San Luis, and Bayate. Due to the severe restrictions the Spanish implemented after the Ten Years' War, weapons were difficult to obtain. However, little by little, the insurgent guerilla forces within the country stole arms from the Spanish, creating an unlikely but deadly force.

In 1894, three ships, the *Lagonda*, the *Almadis*, and the *Baracoa*, attempted to deliver needed weapons to Cuba. Two were stopped by American authorities, but one got through.

Events then unfolded quickly. In 1895, guerilla troops landed onshore in the *Baracoa*. This didn't go unnoticed by the Spanish forces, who increased their numbers to nearly 100,000 men. José Martí was killed upon the landing—a blow to the Cuban patriotic cause. However, Máximo Gómez, who had fought valiantly in the Ten Years' War, came forward and was joined by Antonio Maceo. The war started in the Oriente province on the eastern side of the island. By September 1895, under the leadership of Salvador Cisneros and Bartolomé Masó, the Jimaguayú Constitution was written and approved.

The Cubans faced General Valeriano Weyler, the commander of the Spanish royalist forces. He was cruel and non-discriminating, killing civilians as well as rebel soldiers, earning him the nickname "The Butcher." Some have estimated that Weyler and his forces killed about 10 percent of Cuba's population. The Spanish herded non-combatants into other cities, resulting in a loss of property and the loss of lives, as the living conditions were inhumane. This encouraged the civilians to join the rebels, something that surprised Weyler.

In late 1896, Antonio Maceo, second in command to Gómez, was killed in Havana. The rebels struggled onward, despite the loss of another influential leader. However, a steady supply of weapons was lost due to America's prohibition of the export of weapons for the war effort in Cuba. Yet the courageous Cubans refused to give up, despite the odds. At the Battle of La Reforma, they even forced the surrender of the Spanish forces.

In 1898, riots were common in the Havana area, and the city was considered unsafe for foreigners. The United States became concerned for its citizens who were living in Havana, mostly for business reasons, and sent a battleship, the USS *Maine*, to act as a form of protection. On February 15th, 1898, an explosion blew from inside the ship, killing 260 people. A subsequent military investigation yielded no culprit, but yellow journalism was quick to point the finger at the Spanish, claiming that a bomb had been put on board. Modern-day investigations believe the explosion was caused by a coal bunker fire, which easily spread due to the ship's faulty design. However, the case of the sinking of the USS *Maine* has not been officially solved.

William McKinley, the US president at the time, did not want to enter the war but stepped in to help alleviate some of the brutal tactics the Spanish used. First of all, he insisted that residents return to their homes, and he also offered to negotiate with the independence fighters. The rebels weren't interested in dealing with the United States, so the matter was held in abeyance for the time being.

The Role of the Press

Many of the Spanish atrocities that occurred in Cuba during the years leading up to the year 1898 were recorded in American newspapers. While many of the stories about the cruelty of the Spanish overlords were true, many were not. This practice of presenting fiction as fact in order to arouse sentiment is called "yellow journalism." In fact, the president of Hearst Publications, William Randolph Hearst, was once quoted as having told a reporter, "You furnish the pictures, and I'll furnish the war." Neither McKinley nor the speaker of the house, Thomas Reed, were in favor of going to war on behalf of Cuba, but the voice of the people eventually prevailed. Reluctantly, McKinley presented the issue to US Congress on April 11th, which voted in favor of a war with Spain over Cuba.

The Spanish-American War

On April 25th, Congress formally declared war. Wisely, McKinley specified that the purpose of this war was not to annex Cuba but to end its civil war and help Cuba establish independence. The Teller Amendment, which was passed along with the war resolution, stated, "The island of Cuba is, and by right should be free and independent." Thus, the Cuban War for Independence transformed into the Spanish-American War.

The Battle of Guantánamo Bay

From June 6th to June 10th, 1898, a full-scale naval and land battle was engaged between the coalition of the American and Cuban forces against the Spanish. The USS *Marblehead*, the USS *St Louis*, and the USS *Yankee* blockaded the harbor. On land, the Cuban insurgents gained control of the Western coast of the bay. When the Spanish ships sailed down to meet them, they quickly retreated, ascertaining that they were outgunned.

The Spanish had a fort on land near the harbor on McCalla Hill. However, the pommeling from the guns of the USS *Marblehead* soon wiped the fort out. Once control was maintained there, the cable lines were cut, and the Spanish were unable to communicate with each other.

The Battle of San Juan Hill

A little over a mile outside Santiago was San Juan Hill, which was held by the Spanish. The American forces readied themselves for the treacherous climb up the hill, which would make them quite vulnerable to the Spanish, as they had the advantage. The 2nd and 10th Infantry Regiments of the 2nd Brigade made their way toward the Spanish lines at the far left. A young lieutenant named Jules Ord asked General Hamilton Hawkins for permission to lead the charge. Seeing the extreme difficulty of that task, he responded, "I will not ask for volunteers, I will not give permission and I will not refuse it. God bless you and good luck!"

One by one, the American units moved up the hill. They were backed up by powerful Gatling guns, which were intended to deflect the enemy troops rather than kill them. The American soldiers were successful, and just after 1 a.m. on July 1st, 1898, the Spanish flag was pulled down from the crest of the hill.

Teddy Roosevelt's Rough Riders

Teddy Roosevelt, who would become the future president of the United States, led his crackerjack troop of Rough Riders up Kettle Hill, which lay alongside San Juan Hill. The Rough Riders were perhaps the most publicized unit of the war and were composed of men from all walks of life. Funnily enough, one of the requirements for being a Rough Rider was being a skilled horseman, yet horses were only brought to Cuba for the officers due to limited space on the boats. The Buffalo Soldiers, an all-black unit, also raced up Kettle Hill alongside the Rough Riders. First Lieutenant "Black Jack" John Pershing recalled the event, saying, "White regiments, black regiments, regulars and Rough Riders, representing the young manhood of the North and the South, fought shoulder to shoulder, unmindful of race or color."

This battle was a decisive victory for the United States, although the Americans lost many more men than the Spanish. The Americans and Spanish not only had to deal with the casualties of war, but they also had to contend with the devastating effects of the heat and yellow fever. More men died on both sides due to disease than the actual conflicts.

On July 3rd, 1898, Spanish Admiral Pascual Cervera y Topete received orders to withdraw. He and the Spanish troops attempted to move westward toward the coast. However, his fleet was fired upon by the US Navy, and many of his ships burned or sank.

The Treaty of Paris

On August 12th, 1898, the United States and Spain signed a peace accord. A more formal treaty took over two months to agree on, but eventually, the Treaty of Paris emerged. As a result of the treaty, the independence of Cuba was formally recognized by Spain. The Treaty of Paris also granted the Philippine Islands, which had a separate conflict that the US was involved in, Puerto Rico, and Guam to the US. The Spanish Empire basically disintegrated with one fell swoop, and it was the start of the US becoming a world power.

The West Indies

The term "West Indies" originated in the 15th century when Christopher Columbus was searching for a quicker route to India without going around South Africa and the Cape of Good Hope. The first landmasses he hit when he sailed west from Spain were today's Bahama Islands, located northwest of Cuba. Over time, Europeans began referring to the region as the West Indies in order to differentiate between the East Indies.

Back in Columbus's day, the existence of the continent of North America was unknown to European travelers. Columbus called the island he landed on San Salvador, but the indigenous people he found there called it Guanahani. The people there were the Lokono, who belonged to a larger family of tribes called the Arawak.

The people Columbus found in the Bahamas were from the same racial group as those in Cuba, the Taíno, who were also a subgroup of the Arawak. Scholars have two theories as to their origin—the Amazon Basin or the Andes Mountains in South America. The Arawaks settled in Puerto Rico and were scattered on some of the other islands of the West Indies as well.

Another culture that inhabited this island region was the Island Caribs, who may have been related to the Mainland Caribs, or the Kalina. The Island Caribs settled in Cuba and some of the other Caribbean islands. Geneticists and researchers have indicated that the Island Caribs have a different ancestry than that of the Arawaks. The Island Caribs, it is believed, migrated there from northeastern South America, Trinidad, Tobago, Barbados, the Windward and Leeward Islands, and the island of Domenica.

The people of the Caribbean islands lived in villages with huts placed in a circle. The larger circular areas, or plazas, sometimes were shaped like oblongs or squares. They were used for ceremonies or ball games.

The males fished or hunted, while the women engaged in agriculture. Everyone was expected to work, and each had their own prescribed tasks to perform in support of the community. Socially, the communities had nobles and commoners and were headed by a chief, or a *cacique*, for each familial subgroup.

The people consumed fish, fruit, vegetables, and meat. No large mammals were present on the islands, so the people ate lizards, turtles, dogs, birds, and even earthworms. They grew cassava, which was very common in South America as well. Corn, squash, beans, peppers, and nuts were also eaten.

Their religions varied, but the one that is most known is the Taíno religion. Yúcahu Maórocoti was the god of creation, who looked over the growth of the cassava. Attabeira was the goddess of the waters. Guabancex was the goddess of storms. She brought with her thunder and wind. The word juracán represented the combination of thunder and wind, which is the etymological root of the word "hurricane." Carved stone and wood statues of these gods were found in Hispaniola and Jamaica.

Columbus described the kindness and peacefulness of the Arawak people in his journal, which was something he took advantage of more and more as time passed:

> They traded with us and gave us everything they had, with good will. They took delight in pleasing us. They are very gentle and without knowledge of what is evil, nor do they murder or stead. They love their neighbors as themselves, and they have the sweetest talk in the word, and are gentle and always laughing.

Spanish Colonization

Soon after Columbus give his report on the Caribbean Islands, Spain began to claim them, starting in 1493 and ending in 1530. Some of the more well-known territories they conquered included Hispaniola, Jamaica, Puerto Rico, the Bahamas, Trinidad, and the

Lesser Antilles. Word raced around Europe of the riches the New World held. The Spanish were incredibly cruel to the native population, killing, torturing, and enslaving them. When there was insufficient manpower to mine for metals, they began importing African slaves.

In the late 16th century, there was a reduction of manpower to conduct the lucrative trade routes from Central America to Europe. Pirates and privateers besieged ships that were supposed to transport silver and gold back to the home countries. A privateer is a "pirate," who was often hired by a nation to raid the ships of another country. One of the most notorious privateers was Sir Francis Drake. Queen Elizabeth I of England even encouraged and supported him. One of the raids Drake conducted was the capture of the Spanish Silver Train, which was used to transport precious metals back to Seville. In March 1573, Drake attacked the train at the port of Nombre de Dios near Darien, in the colony of Panama, and stole the gold. He was unable to steal the silver as well because it was simply too heavy to safely transport across the Atlantic. Sir Henry Newbolt, a 16th-century poet, recorded the exploit in the first stanza of his verse called "Drake's Drum":

> Drake he's in his hammock an' a thousand mile away,
>
> (Capten, art tha sleepin' there below?)
>
> Slung atween the round shot in Nombre Dios Bay,
>
> An' dreamin' arl the time o' Plymouth Hoe.
>
> Yarnder lumes the island, yarnder lie the ships,
>
> Wi' sailor lads a-dancin' heel-an'-toe,
>
> An' the shore-lights flashin, an' the night-tide dashin'
>
> He sees et arl so plainly as he saw et long ago.

"Arl" is an old English term for an isle, and "hoe" means a highland. Terms like "buccaneers" and "swashbucklers" soon came into use and took on a more romantic meaning, becoming the meat of literature and wild tales of adventures on the high seas. The European countries of France, Denmark, Norway, and Great Britain all had colonies in the Caribbean, and they began competing with each other to see who would come out on top. The late 16th century through the early 17th century was a bloodthirsty era, during which greed ruled politics.

French corsairs (privateers) attacked Spanish ships at sea in search of the treasures they carried back to Europe. Ports and villages were sacked and destroyed. France and the Holy Roman Empire went to war in 1521, and the hostilities spread to the Western Hemisphere. The conflict took on a religious significance, as it pitted the Roman Catholics against the Protestants. As a result, France and Britain carried their centuries-old rivalry to the New World.

Between 1612 and 1672, the British created colonies on the islands of Bermuda, Barbados, Nevis, Antigua, Anguilla, Montserrat, Jamaica, and Tortola. France and Britain split the island of St. Kitts. The French took possession of Martinique, St. Barts, St. Croix, St. Lucia, Grenada, Saint-Domingue (Haiti), Tortuga, and St. Vincent. The Dutch took over St. Martin, Sint Eustatius, Saba, Curacao, Bonaire, Aruba, Tobago, Anegada, and Virgin Gorda.

Slavery

From 1662 until 1807, Great Britain shipped in three million Africans to work on the new sugar plantations in the West Indies. Harvesting sugarcane was a very labor-intensive process. The British sailors forced them to lay down sideways in the cargo holds of the ships, body to body. The slave masters earned a great deal of money selling the Africans. As can be expected, there was a great deal of cruelty and abuse toward the blacks who came to the Caribbean.

There were countless rebellions, the larger of which were Tacky's Rebellion in Jamaica in 1760, the Haitian Revolution in 1791, and Fédon's Rebellion in Grenada in 1795. Naval warfare accelerated when the governors of the various islands passed decrees legalizing the detainment and seizure of ships from other country's fleets. In

1791, Governor John Orde of Domenica passed an order, which said, in part:

> Whereas several Gangs of Slaves, with-in this Island, are in a State of Insurrection, and may receive great Succor or Assistance from an improper Communication of Foreign Vessels with the Out-bays of this Island. I have, therefore, thought fit, by this my Proclamation, to call upon and require all Magistrates...to detain all Foreign Vessels that may be discovered landing or taking any Thing from any of the Out-bays; and to deliver up such vessels to any Commander his Majesty's Ships of War.

Sugar, Cotton, and Coffee Plantations

Sugar was a highly desirable luxury in Europe. The colonists set up sugar plantations throughout the islands and enslaved the indigenous population, who mainly harvested it. The work didn't merely consist of just harvesting the cane; it also required masons, coopers, joiners, and metalworkers to manufacture and maintain the barrels and provide the transportation of the product. Saint-Domingue (Haiti) was the greatest exporter of sugar.

Besides sugar, the islands grew tobacco, cotton, and indigo plants. Indigo created a blue dye that was very popular in Europe.

Haitian Rebellion and Independence

Haiti, formerly known as Saint-Domingue, was a French-owned colony. There was a strict social caste system in place. There were three main groups: the whites, free persons of color, and black slaves. The free persons of color were the children of white slave owners and their slaves. They were given more privileges than the slaves, like land ownership, but there were laws in place to restrict them from adopting too many of the cultural practices of the whites. The slaves outnumbered the other groups ten to one.

Back in the 16th century, when African slaves started arriving on the island in great numbers, Christian missionaries converted many of the slaves. This led to a blending of religions, with the Yoruba people, who were brought to Haiti in great numbers, being one of the major contributors. This blending of traditions evolved into what is called Vodou (also spelled as Voodoo, although those who practice the religion today avoid this spelling). Some of the slaves eventually escaped and moved to the hills, where they sought ways to start rebellions.

In 1791, France was in the throes of the French Revolution. People there fought for the liberty of the masses and rose up against the monarchy. It was a struggle for freedom, which influenced other French colonies. In the summer of 1791, thousands of slaves rose up, and they managed to place the entire northern province under their control. Within weeks, the number of slaves rebelling reached into the hundreds of thousands. Although the white plantation owners were expecting a revolution to arise at some point, they weren't quite prepared for the scale on which it took place. In 1792, the slaves controlled an impressive third of the island. This led to the National Assembly in Paris to send in outside help, Léger-Félicité Sonthonax. Sonthonax and his men were meant to put down the slave rebellions, but they were also there to guarantee the rights and liberties of the free blacks and those of mixed-race, who were called *gens de couleur* ("people of color"). Sonthonax soon abolished slavery in the northern province, which went against his original purpose for going to Haiti. By 1793, Sonthonax declared all the slaves to be free on the island. He played a key role in the abolition of slavery in all French possessions in 1794.

In 1793, France and Britain were at war with each other. The white colonists sought the help of the British, believing that if the island was under British rule, they could continue owning slaves. Spain soon entered the war as well and sent over its forces, who joined up with the slaves to fight for independence.

A free black man by the name of Toussaint Louverture was responsible for the alliance between Spain and the Haitian rebels. Over time, he became known as a noted leader of the revolution, and he is perhaps the most well-known of the leaders today. Eventually, Louverture and the Spanish parted ways, for reasons that are not fully understood today, and Louverture turned back to the French once the abolition of slavery officially went into effect in France. It did not take long for Louverture to force the Spanish off the island.

In southern Saint-Domingue, an accomplished military man by the name of General André Rigaud formed a mulatto separatist movement, which fought against the troops of Louverture. The conflict escalated into a battle on many fronts: that of the blacks against the mulattoes who wanted to retain their newly gained privileges, that of the blacks and the mulattoes against the whites, and that of France against the native-born people of Saint-Domingue.

In 1801, Louverture declared himself to be the governor-for-life and that Saint-Domingue would be a sovereign black state. When Napoleon Bonaparte, who had taken control of France by this point, heard this, he immediately sent over troops to assert his own power on the island. In 1802, the French landed on the island, but capturing Louverture proved to be harder than they expected. The Haitians moved ahead of the French, employing scorched-earth tactics and leaving nothing behind for the French to use. The French didn't give up easily, though, and both sides engaged in heavy fighting, with both being shocked at how violent just the initial battles were. In late April, the French informed Louverture that he would be given his freedom if he gave his remaining troops to the French. In May, Louverture realized that neither side was making much progress and agreed to those terms.

Unfortunately for Louverture, it was just a ploy. The French arrested him, and he was shipped off to France, where he died in prison. Before his death, Toussaint Louverture said these prophetic words, "In overthrowing me you have to cut down in St. Domingue only the trunk of the tree of liberty; it will spring up again from the roots, for they are many and they are deep."

Louverture's protégé, Jean-Jacques Dessalines, capitulated to the French and was made a governor. However, despite these setbacks, the rebellion continued. When it became clear that the French planned on reinstating slavery, a whole new wave of resistance broke out. The French were quite harsh to the Haitians, treating them brutally and subjecting them to sadistic torture and death. In the fall of 1802, Dessalines switched sides once more. The French had been decimated by yellow fever, not to mention the harsh tactics the Haitians used, especially by Dessalines. In November 1803, the pivotal Battle of Vertières was fought, and the Haitian rebels defeated the French. In early 1804, Dessalines declared independence, with himself leading the nation as its new emperor.

Conclusion

In this book, you have experienced the magnificent tapestry that is the Western Hemisphere. The fight for independence is something that binds the continents of North America and South America together, but their cultures and the history that follows are entirely different.

As time drove onward, South America has seen the rise and fall of several different revolutions and dictatorships. Democracy is now widespread there, although there are many cases of corruption, and the various cultures of the many different countries are thriving. North America took a different path altogether. In Mexico, the Mexican Revolution, which lasted from 1910 until 1920, transformed the culture and government of Mexico entirely, bringing it a stability that was not seen in South America. Canada remains a progressive power in the world, although Canada is still technically a part of the British Commonwealth. The United States grew to become a world power, rivaling other powerful countries on the international stage. The countries of North America have faced their fair share of corruption as well, along with many rebellions of their own. The various cultures of these three North American nations, not to mention the various other cultures of Central America and the Caribbean, play a large role on the global stage.

It is crazy to think of how far these countries have come since the arrival of Christopher Columbus in 1492. But before Columbus, Cortés, and Magellan even arrived, there were many thriving civilizations. The Aztecs, the Maya, the Inca, and the many Native American tribes in the US and Canada were all here before the Europeans set foot on the shores of the Americas, and while some tribes are entirely extinct now, many are still here today. There have been recent efforts to keep their cultures alive, without the interference of European cultures, with a large focus on language and stories.

As the territory of the Americas is large, so is its history. It is perhaps too much to cover in such a short book, but hopefully, you will leave with questions of your own that you can more fully explore. As time goes on, the countries of the Americas will continue to face challenges that their people must overcome. But hopefully, the people will do as their ancestors had done in the past and come together as one to address the issues they face.

Here's another book by Captivating History that you might be interested in

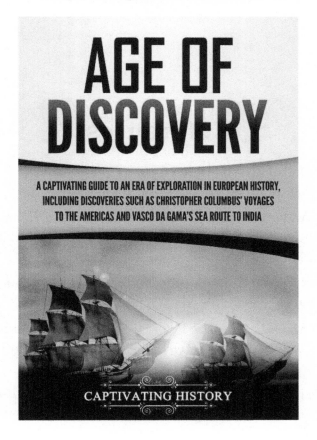

References

"US-Cuba Relations." Retrieved from
https://www.cfr.org/backgrounder/us-cuba-relations

DePalma, Anthony (2006). *The Man Who Invented Fidel: Cuba, Castro, and Herbert L. Matthews of The New York Times* (1st ed.). New York: Public Affairs

Castañeda, Jorge G. (1998). *Compañero: The life and Death of Che Guevara* (1st Vintage Books ed.). Vintage Books.

Kirk, John M. and McKenna, Peter (1997). *Canada-Cuba Relations: The Other Good Neighbor Policy.* University Press of Florida. 207 pp.

Paterson, Thomas G. (1994). *Contesting Castro: The United States and the Triumph of the Cuban Revolution.* Oxford University Press. 352 pp.

Carlson, J. B. "Lodestone Compass: Chinese or Olmec Primacy?" Science 05 Sept 1975.

"Pyramids in Latin America." Retrieved from
https://www.history.com/topics/ancient-history/pyramids-in-latin-america

"The Decline of the Olmec Civilization." Retrieved from https://www.thoughtco.com/the-decline-of-the-olmec-civilization-2136291

"Artifacts and Ancient Writings: The Popol Vuh." https://www.ancient-origins.net/artifacts-ancient-writings/popol-vuh-sacred-narrative-maya-creation-002893

"Popol Vuh: The Sacred Narrative of Maya Creation." Retrieved from https://www.ancient-origins.net/artifacts-ancient-writings/popol-vuh-sacred-narrative-maya-creation-002893

Shorn, M. Don (2011). *Gardens of the Elder Gods.* Amazon Services.

Chamberlain, R. S. (1948). *The Conquest and Colonization of Yucatan 1517-1550.* Carnegie Institution.

Coe, M. D, (1967). *The Maya.* Thames & Hudson.

Fieldman, L. H. (2000). *Lost Shores, Forgotten People: Spanish Explorations of the Southeast Mayan Lowlands.* Duke University Press.

Sharer, R. J., & Traxler, Loa P. *The Ancient Maya.* Stanford.

Diaz del Castillo, B. (1963). *The Conquest of New Spain.* Penguin Classics.

Diaz del Castillo, B., Maudslay, A.F. (2004). *The Discovery and Conquest of Mexico.*

Made in the USA
Monee, IL
19 June 2021